WORKING IN FOUNDATIONS

Career Patterns
of
Women and Men

Teresa Jean Odendahl
Elizabeth Trocolli Boris
Arlene Kaplan Daniels

The Foundation Center

ABW 6441- 9/2

Printed and bound in the United States of America

The publication of this book was made possible by a grant from
the Russell Sage Foundation. The project on career patterns
in philanthropy was initiated by the Research Committee of
Women and Foundations/Corporate Philanthropy with funding from the Russell Sage Foundation and the John Hay Whitney Foundation.

Library of Congress Cataloging in Publication Data

Odendahl, Teresa Jean.
   Working in Foundations.

   Bibliography: p.
   Includes index.
   1. Endowments -- United States -- Officials and employees.
I. Boris, Elizabeth T.   II. Daniels, Arlene Kaplan,
1930-   . III. Title.
HV97.A3034 1985   361.7'632'02373   84-60649

Contents

List of Tables

Foreword

Ten years ago over 80 foundation women gathered for an informal luncheon at the Council on Foundations annual meeting in Chicago to discuss common concerns. That meeting served as a catalyst for a number of efforts over the ensuing years to improve the status of women in the foundation field and increase the funding of programs benefiting women and girls. Among early efforts was the formation of the Planning Committee for Women and Foundations, a group of 15 female foundation trustees and staff, which began a fact-gathering and analysis process in late 1975 to determine the status of women in the field and the barriers to funding for women's programs. Operating on an informal basis and with limited funds, the Committee reviewed available research, conducted interviews with foundation leaders, and met with representatives of women's organizations. As a member of the Committee, I conducted a survey (438 foundations participated) which yielded additional data: only 19 percent of foundation trustees were women and 29 percent of foundation professional staff were female. While 45 percent of the foundations surveyed had provided support for programs directed to the needs of women and girls in 1974–75, most funders stated that such programs were either outside their program areas, a low priority, or that the proposals received raised doubts about the ability of the organizations to carry out the programs.

The Committee saw that a formal education and advocacy effort was needed. The incorporation of Women and Foundations/Corporate Philanthropy, Inc. (WAF/CP) followed, and with it an expanding network of women and men in the philanthropic field committed to the full and equal participation of women in philanthropy and equity in funding of programs for women and girls.

In 1981, the Research Committee of WAF/CP began to develop plans for a project to examine the progress of women in the field, and to look at their world of work and that of their male colleagues. We were fortunate in securing the *pro bono* services of Teresa Odendahl, then Acting Executive Director of the Business and Professional Women's Foundation, who drafted the research proposal. The addition of Elizabeth Boris, Director of Research at the Council on Foundations, and Arlene Kaplan Daniels, Professor of Sociology at Northwestern University, strengthened the project team. Alida Brill of the Russell Sage Foundation helped refine and shape the proposal which led to funding by the Russell Sage Foundation. Additional support by the John Hay Whitney Foundation, WAF/CP, and the Council on Foundations, augmented by the donation of many of the services provided by the research team members themselves, enabled the project to begin.

The resulting book, *Working in Foundations: Career Patterns of Women and Men*, is the most complete picture available of the world of work for women and men in the foundation field. And, in a real sense, the study describes a microcosm of the world of work in general. Women earn 59 cents for every dollar men earn; so do women who work in foundations. Women in the workforce need increased education and training, support structures, and the opportunity for expanded work experience; so do women who work in foundations. And, in those cases where all factors are equal, the wage gap persists; for women in general and for women in foundations.

Though there are encouraging signs of progress, the task for foundations that was articulated some ten years ago remains: barriers to the full participation of women in the foundation field and in the workforce at large must be eliminated. This study provides the case for continuing commitment and action.

Leeda Marting

Preface

The research reported in this book grew out of our personal and scholarly interests in the status of women, as well as our connections with the foundation field. Although over half of all American women work outside the home, most hold low-paying jobs and put in a "double day." Women employed by private grantmaking organizations are relatively privileged in comparison to those in other occupations. Yet it seems that even in an elite field women's economic contributions are undervalued.

Since this manuscript was written, the Council on Foundations published the *1984 Foundation Management Report*. This new data permits us to take another look at the relative status and salary levels of men and women in foundation philanthropy. The situation has changed little since 1982, lending us additional confidence in the data that were used for our analysis.

The proportion of respondents by size and type of foundation vary one percent at most from 1982, although an additional 87 foundations responded to the survey.

There were 99 women CEOs (27 percent) in 1984, compared to 72 (26 percent) in 1982. In all, 2,658 (68 percent) of foundation staff are women, compared to 1,500 (66 percent) in 1982. The proportion of women on foundation boards remained constant at 23 percent, but there were 1,099 women trustees reported in 1984 compared to 834 in 1982.

An analysis of relative salaries of women and men in professional positions reveals little change from 1982. The smaller the foundation, the more likely that the salaries of women CEOs will be substantially less than their male counterparts. Taken as a group, women CEOs have salaries that average $38,978, compared to $69,884 for men, 56 cents for every dollar earned by men. As in 1982, the ratio of women's to men's salaries is less extreme at the program officer level where women make 70 cents for every dollar earned by men. In other professional positions, the ratio is 60 cents for every dollar.

A number of people and organizations helped us with this endeavor, especially those persons we interviewed and the foundations that cooperated with us in the study. Leeda Marting and Alida Brill deserve special thanks. Many in the foundation field have thought about the issues we examine here, but Dr. Marting acted on her ideas. As Chair of the Research Committee of Women and Foundations/Corporate Philanthropy, she served as the broker who saw the project through from inception to completion. Dr. Brill was our program officer at the Russell Sage Foundation, the major funder of the study. Like many women in similar positions, her advocacy, encouragement, and support were essential. The John Hay Whitney Foundation, under the directorship of Leeda Marting, contributed a small grant to the cause as well.

The research was sponsored by Women and Foundations/Corporate Philanthropy, and they underwrote our expenses in the developmental phase. All the members of WAF/CP deserve credit, but we wish to express appreciation to the leaders who believed in the project and raised the money for it, particularly Jean Fairfax, Jing Lyman, Martha Golensky, and Joanne Hayes.

The Department of Anthropology at the University of Colorado provided space and services, without charging overhead to the project. Dr. Gottfried Lang extended his friendship as well as part of his office to us. Fran Snow, the administrative assistant in Anthropology at CU, and David Greene, who was then Chairman, arranged all this and were always extremely helpful to their former graduate student, Terry Odendahl, to whom they had no official obligation. Anne Stockholm, the research assistant, was creative, diligent, funny, and resourceful. Terry gives her personal thanks.

In addition, the Council on Foundations, under the direction of Eugene Struckhoff and then James Joseph, was a partner in the study almost from the beginning. They helped provide entry to the foundation community and, most importantly, lent their Director of Research, Elizabeth Boris, and her data to the study. They also contributed her travel and computer time. Jane Dustan, Chair, and members of the Council on Foundations Research Committee, as well as other Council staff provided comments and encouragement. We express personal and very special thanks to Carol Hooper, Research Associate, who worked with us throughout the project.

David Kantor, Nelson Rosenbaum, and Marie Eldridge all offered counsel and made suggestions regarding the interpretation and presentation of statistics. Robert Mutah was responsible for the programming at the University of Colorado, and Chris de Fontenay did the programming at the Brookings Institution.

The final revisions on our manuscript were completed at Yale University's Program on Non-Profit Organizations, under the direction of Paul DiMaggio and John Simon. Peter Hall and Craig Jenkins, scholars in the program, also made invaluable comments. The book was typed and re-typed by Marilyn Mandell. We also wish to thank Thomas Buckman, President of The Foundation Center, for his support of this project, and Pat Read, Director of Publications at The Foundation Center, for her fine editing and professional approach to the publication process.

Finally, and most importantly, we thank our families and friends: Jay, Paul and David Boris; Richard Daniels; Kent Harvey, Kevin Hearne, Dan and Elaine Oran, Pam and John Rifkin, all coped with our absorption in the subject by long discussions of the issues and editing help. Their patience and support is a continuing source of gratification to us.

While we appreciate and acknowledge the support of all of these organizations and individuals, the authors take sole responsibility for the contents of this book.

Teresa Odendahl
Elizabeth Boris
Arlene Kaplan Daniels
March, 1985

1

Introduction to Foundation Philanthropy and the Career Patterns Study

Foundations are a small but important part of the philanthropic sector in the United States. Often characterized as uniquely American institutions, they assumed their current form and flourished along with the profit motive of modern industrialism. Capitalist enterprise allowed the accumulation of vast personal fortunes, and a few industrialists and their heirs funded various benevolent activities. In the early part of the twentieth century, Andrew Carnegie, Margaret Olivia Sage, and John D. Rockefeller, Sr., set a precedent among the wealthy by promoting grantmaking and endowing foundations to fund programs, institutions, and research that seemed able to help solve social problems or improve the quality of life.

Today there are about 23,800 foundations distributing over $4.5 billion annually to a wide variety of philanthropic endeavors. Approximately 1,500 private grantmaking institutions employ paid staff members. This book examines the nature of grantmaking work, the career paths of foundation employees, and the status of women as compared with men in the field.

Private Grantmaking

Independent foundations, the most common grantmaking organizations, are established by individuals and families. Contributions usually form an endowment that generates the income for giving. Community foundations are publicly supported; they receive contributions from a variety of donors. They serve a local region or town, and are legally required to have governing boards that are representative of the community. Company-sponsored foundations award grants with funds donated by a parent corporation. Company executives and owners are generally on the board or distribution committee. Operating foundations[1] provide direct services or conduct research; grantmaking is not a primary activity.

Foundation trustees range from donors, their family members or heirs, business associates and friends, to corporate officers, and in some cases dignitaries or experts in particular funding areas. Since the 1970s, there has been an increase in the number of women and minorities who serve as trustees, but white men still dominate foundation boards. This is particularly true of the largest private grantmaking organizations. The larger an independent foundation, the lower the proportion of women on the board (Boris and Hooper 1982).

Grantmaking has always been clouded by an image of the wealthy family or elite clique arbitrarily dispensing gifts. This image is reinforced by the fact that most foundations are vehicles for family philanthropy and do not have employees. When there are paid staff, it is not surprising that trustees look for individuals with whom they feel comfortable, who understand their point of view, and who reflect their values. In fact, foundation employees, and particularly chief executive officers (CEOs), often have personal attributes and backgrounds like those of the board members for whom they work.

The highest ranking staff position in the foundation community is the CEO, who usually has the title of president or executive director. An overwhelming majority of foundation executives are white men. Most are middle-aged or older. In 1982, only 26 percent of all CEOs were women (see Table 1; Boris and Hooper 1982; Boris, Unkle, and Hooper 1980). A CEO is often the sole employee, a generalist responsible for all day-to-day operations of a grantmaking organization. At larger foundations, however, an executive administers the activities of other staff members with specialized functions. As chief staff officers, CEOs have authority over other employees, but they are accountable to a board of trustees.

Foundation executives and staff members implement the policies of the board, which is responsible for exercising financial oversight, developing grantmaking criteria and overall policies, hiring a CEO, considering employee recommendations on particular projects, and ultimately deciding whether or not to fund proposals. The staff review grant applications, determine how well they fit board policy, investigate applicants' ability to complete projects, and prepare formal written recommendations for the board. Some boards seem to rubber-stamp employee recommendations; others are active participants in the daily operations of the foundation. Boards of the smaller family foundations are usually more involved in the day-to-day operations of the foundation than are

---

[1] Our emphasis in this study is on grantmaking organizations rather than operating foundations.

Table 1. Foundation Positions by Gender and Race

Position	Women*	Men	Minorities*	White
Chief Executive Officers	72	200	3	269
	26%	74%	1%	99%
Executives	109	173	21	255
	39%	61%	8%	92%
Program Staff	189	181	49	315
	51%	49%	13%	87%
Other Professionals	127	99	18	204
	56%	44%	8%	92%
Total	497	653	91	1043
	43%	57%	8%	92%

* Some respondents did not specify gender or minority status of employees.
SOURCE: *1982 Compensation and Benefits Survey* conducted by the Council on Foundations.

the boards of the larger foundations. CEOs of many of the smaller foundations have limited decision-making authority.

Although staff members often have substantial influence, employees usually do not control foundation funds. But sometimes they assume that they have control. One staff member said:

> You begin to think it is your own money, the longer you are in foundation work. And that means that you get a little more restive about what the board decides. And whether or not they know what they are doing, you want more and more discretion. You want more and more authority. You begin to think you know everything about everything.

However, CEOs and other staff members serve at the pleasure of the board: employees have to be sensitive to the board's role. It is clear why trustees may want to choose executives who resemble themselves; they can respect the judgments and find it easier to trust the recommendations of those with whom they share some common perspectives.

Many foundation employees think of themselves as generalists without any particular qualifications. A CEO we interviewed presented the "wisdom" of the field: "The only qualification for philanthropy is common sense." And yet boards tend to hire CEOs with advanced degrees from elite institutions, and CEOs tend to hire program officers with equivalent educational backgrounds.

There may be no specific training that is seen as necessary to do the work of philanthropy, but there does seem to be a faith in the efficacy of academic credentials. In addition to the widely held belief in the value of advanced education, the ability to write clearly and speak well are seen as important. Many observers of the foundation field argue that few funding programs are effectively managed without staff members, but there is no consensus on the skills required for the work.

Despite the often amorphous nature of funding criteria, "professional" grantmaking rests on the assumption that rational funding decisions are possible. Foundation staff members are supposed to judge the merits of grant proposals and program ideas impartially, based on board policy. In practice, since criteria are usually not explicit, determinations are actually based on employees' values and preferences within the range delimited by the board. Nonetheless, the form of impartial, rational decision-making is carefully preserved through review and consultation procedures.

Professionalism

Foundation philanthropy is a developing field that is slowly becoming more professional. Private grantmaking organizations have been hiring more paid staff members to administer giving programs. These employees have been seeking to legitimize their occupation as a profession. Among the professional qualities they point to are expertise developed in making judgments and seeing future directions in the grantmaking arena. Part of the impetus to professionalize also includes a concern about the status of the work and the regard that others—such as board members, professionals, and business people—have for those who do it. The desire to upgrade the work and to portray it as somehow special are part of the trend toward "professionalism."[2] This trend is countered to some extent by the fact that generalists without formal training have often undertaken comparable tasks.

Outside the largest foundations, job descriptions are rare and the division of responsibility is often not well defined. CEOs of small foundations usually manage the entire range of programmatic and administrative duties, while program officers may be responsible for proposal review, some of the management, or secretarial tasks in addition to other duties. Similarly, administrative assistants in small grantmaking organizations sometimes perform duties that would qualify them as office managers or even program officers in larger foundations.

Women in Foundations

Employment in foundations has been increasing concurrently with female labor force participation. Charitable work has always attracted women for several reasons. First, the ideology of doing good fits into expected notions of women's aspirations and interests. There is also a compatibility of the ideology of good

---

[2] That is, the effort to achieve higher status for an occupation through the trappings of a profession: codes of ethics, membership societies, journals, and certification of practitioners are examples of the strategies used (Collins 1975; Hughes 1958; Wilensky 1964).

work with stereotypes of feminine qualities, especially for upper-class women, who may share many conventional ideas about gender stereotypes with the men of their class (Ostrander 1984). The notion that women should devote some of their time helping others has had a long tradition. Both upper- and middle-class women not employed outside the home have often volunteered their services to community, cultural, and religious causes.

When foundations were created with family funds, administrative duties were considered suitable for female relatives. In addition, donors were concerned that costs be kept low to reserve most of the funds for the cause. Accordingly, women who were willing to accept low pay, or who worked for nothing, were considered ideal foundation employees. Service to others generally rates the lowest economic return; and service occupations have become almost synonymous with low-paying occupations. But occasionally expectations that women will be more supportive and nurturant can create positions for them. This view, combined with the expectation that women are likely to be cheaper to hire, sometimes provides them with special niches of opportunity.

While the foundation field may be such a niche of opportunity for women, historical and structural constraints face those who wish to pursue careers in philanthropy. Although women have traditionally organized and run charitable and reform programs, the president, professor, or administrator from an elite university is still the preferred executive for many of the nation's largest foundations. Since patterns of academic employment and promotion still favor males for high-ranking positions in that setting, few women have been able to follow this path to the leadership of foundations.

Large private foundations were never havens for salaried women, who probably played a greater role in managing smaller family foundations. The first large foundations deliberately set out to differentiate themselves from "lady bountiful" charity. They focused instead on "scientific philanthropy" that searched for root causes of social problems, employing the business methods and corporate form that had proven so successful in their commercial endeavors. Many of these early foundations supported research at prestigious universities, spending much of their largesse on facilities and underwriting major programs (Rosenberg 1982).

Initial foundation staff members were often business colleagues of the donor, and later were drawn from among leading figures in elite educational institutions, often after a tour in high-level government posts. These career paths of business, academia, government, and foundation service virtually excluded women. Corporations rarely employed women as executives, and most of the prestigious colleges and universities did not hire women except at the lowest ranks. While it has been possible for women to earn advanced degrees at some institutions since the turn of the century, few women were hired as faculty members outside of women's colleges, much less as heads of departments, full professors, or high-level administrators. Women who were employed by universities were rarely promoted above entry positions, except in fields such as home economics, and were paid much less than their male colleagues of comparable backgrounds. The federal government also denied qualified women high-level positions, which were reserved for men (Rossiter 1982).

As a result of institutional practices that contribute to discriminatory educational and hiring patterns, most foundations were staffed by white males at the program and policy levels until the early 1970s. There were exceptions, chiefly women hired on projects related to women or children. Women worked for pay or volunteered to perform the routine clerical tasks of the foundation. Much of the day-to-day work was performed by women who were largely excluded from "professional" positions.

Foundation Research

The only major study of foundation employees found that professionals were primarily white men (Zurcher and Dustan 1972). Zurcher and Dustan dealt with the position of women in the field in one paragraph:

> Only one or two foundations that can be considered of major size have a woman chief executive. There is the usual and frequently hidden discriminatory salary and promotion policy, with the resultant, all too frequently justifiable complaint that women do the work and men reap the kudos and monetary rewards. With token exceptions, the world of the staffed foundation is still a white world and a man's world, and this fact does not appear to cause too serious concern among those who govern and manage foundations. [p. 127]

Of full-time employees, only 17 percent were women. No data were reported for minorities.

Several more recent, although not strictly comparable, surveys have shown increasing numbers of women and minorities in the field. According to Leeda Marting, in 1973 twenty-eight percent of foundation professional staff were women, as compared with 29 percent in 1976. Since then, the Council on Foundations has undertaken a major study of compensation and benefits among foundations every other year. Questions concerning gender were not added to the compensation and benefits survey (*CB Survey*) until 1980, when women were found to comprise 43 percent of all foundation professionals (Boris and Unkle 1981).

Although more women are entering grantmaking, men hold the high-paying jobs, and few women are in top decision-making positions. Those women who are executives tend to work in small foundations. Women comprise 66 percent of the field, but two thirds of them are support staff (Boris and Hooper 1982). If we consider all positions above the support staff level, female foundation professionals earn 59 cents for each dollar made by men (computed from the 1982 *CB Survey* data).

Interview Sample for This Study

The random sample for this exploratory study of women and men in the private grantmaking field was drawn from employees of foundations responding to the 1980 *CB Survey*. The 60 participants selected for the research worked as staff members at 42 foundations located in New York City, the Midwest, or California (see Table 2). We interviewed people who worked as chief executive officers (CEOs), program officers, and administrative assistants (see Table 3), the most commonly held positions in foundations. Because of our interest in the status of women in this occupational area, the sample was designed to overrepresent them. We wanted approximately equal sampling of female and male professionals. However, this aim was not achievable for the category of administrative assistants, since virtually all support personnel are women. Although a few men are employed as administrative assistants at foundations, the job has been stereotyped as a women's position. Occupational segregation by gender is just as prevalent in the foundation world as it is in the larger labor force.

Although the work CEOs perform is comparable, we found significant differences between the 11 women and 16 men we interviewed. Women executives are found at smaller foundations; they tend to be younger than men CEOs, work with more diverse titles, and are less likely to be included as trustees on their foundations' boards. Women CEOs usually have less authority and discretion and earn significantly lower salaries than their male counterparts.

Fifteen of the 23 program officers we interviewed are women. Most are white and in their thirties and forties. Program officers are typically responsible

Table 2. Geographical Distribution (Interview Sample)

	New York City	Midwest	California	Total
Foundations	14	16	12	42
Individual Participants	19	22	19	60

Table 3. Position by Gender (Interview Sample)

	Women	Men	Total
Chief Executive Officer	11	16	27
	34%	67%	45%
Program Officer	15	8	23
	43%	33%	38%
Administrative Assistant	10	0	10
	28%	0%	17%
Total	36	24	60
	60%	40%	100%

for reviewing grant proposals, making recommendations on funding, and monitoring projects which receive financial assistance. The grantmaking duties of program officers at large foundations are similar to those of executive directors at small grantmaking organizations. About 16 percent of all paid foundation personnel are program officers. Almost as many women as men are employed in these positions (Boris and Hooper 1982), but women program officers make much less than men in comparable jobs.

Administrative assistants are highly skilled clerical workers. The coordinating and secretarial duties they perform are essential to the smooth functioning of foundations and other organizations where they are employed. However, such positions are often overlooked in analyses of occupational areas because even the most skilled clerical work is undervalued and tends to be invisible within organizations. (See Kanter 1977a for an analysis of the career limitations for even the most visible and high-ranking executive secretaries; and Charlton 1983 for descriptions of the functions performed by different categories of secretaries within an organization.)

More women than men work at foundations, but most, like administrative assistants, are classified as nonexempt support personnel. Although they have prestigious clerical jobs, administrative assistants generally do not have professional status. The ten administrative assistants who participated in the research are all white women over 30 years of age; a majority are over forty-five. Their salaries range from $10,000 to nearly $30,000 a year.

Focused Interview Method

In conducting this research we used the focused interview method (Lofland 1971; Merton *et al.* 1956). An interview guide structured the discussion (see Appendix 2), although informants were encouraged to talk freely about their experiences. They were invited to become research partners as observers and interpreters of their world. This method is particularly important when, as in this study, a new area is investigated and the participants are likely to have a very real interest in the information collected. In general, this method provides informants an opportunity to express what they experience and how they wish their work to be seen. The length of the interviews, and internal comparisons of the material within them, combined with the statements of employees at all levels of the hierarchy—including the disaffected—also provide grounds for considering this collection of data a reasonable appraisal of the field. Finally, the method provides opportunities to discover new issues, for informants can open additional areas for exploration and help revise topics already considered (Bucher and Stelling 1977).

Interviews were conducted by the authors between March and October 1982. Responses were usually taped and then transcribed verbatim; in some cases, the researcher dictated from notes after the interview was concluded. During the interviews we asked participants to discuss their employment backgrounds and current work situations. We also sought personal and family information. In addition, we were interested in the perspectives of foundation employees on the relation between work and private life. We gave special attention to any issues which might aid in explaining the earnings differential between men and women in the foundation field.

Since our interview sample is small, and findings are based on informants' perceptions of their situations, we undertook additional comparative and statistical analysis of the relevant 1982 *CB Survey* data (429 foundations) as part of this study. Statistical analysis of the 1982 *CB Survey* data is limited by the low number of staff in certain positions. Yet, the survey does provide the most comprehensive information available.

2

The Structure of
Foundation Employment

Private foundations usually have hierarchical staffing arrangements. Rank is shaped like a pyramid, particularly for women. Only a third of the total working population are labeled "professional" as compared with "support" staff. Workplaces are organized along a continuum from extremely bureaucratic and sometimes authoritarian to nearly consensual and democratic. The size of a foundation as well as the policies of boards and management styles of executives affect the overall performance of grantmaking employees and the quality of their interaction.

Employee Relationships with the Board

A central job responsibility, mentioned by all of the CEOs we interviewed and some of the program officers and administrative assistants, is interaction with the board of trustees. The staff-board relationship is crucial to effective foundation operation. Successful foundation management requires good communication and a delicate balance of power between trustees and employees.

Most of the chief executives we interviewed reported "good working relationships" with their boards. CEOs carefully cultivate the respect and trust of their trustees. As a sign of success in this effort, many executives stressed the informal power they have acquired. CEOs may adopt the posture of controlling or at least easily managing the direction of board policy in their comments to us, but they all recognize the importance of managing the delicate balance. The president of a large independent foundation discussed how this process works:

I think there are two sides to this problem of board motivation and board feeling that the staff is taking over. I think that our staff really tries very hard once it understands what the board wants to come up with. So we don't manipulate the board by coming in with marginal things.

While the preceding remarks suggest a sensitivity to the wishes of the board, executives still stress their own authority. This same foundation president focused on providing leadership for the trustees:

My tasks are to help the board formulate its policies, both about the areas in which we make grants, and the ways in which the foundation will operate. The care and feeding of the board, keeping up its motivation, making the board work interesting and rewarding—satisfying—is an important responsibility.

His remarks demonstrate the ambiguity of multifaceted roles: CEOs see themselves as both following and shaping board policy.

However, a woman CEO at another independent foundation described her board functions differently, stressing implementing rather than designing policy. She interacts with the Chair, who directs the activities of the trustees. This executive director commented: "I assist the Chair of the board in deciding which grants will be recommended, and then administering those grants." In this case, the Chair is also the donor of the foundation and personally involved with the grantmaking programs on an almost daily basis.

Another president explained how he worked with his board:

I never go very far in getting out on a limb unless I've talked to my board, or unless I am confident that I have the support of the board. Sometimes I just talk to my Chair, who is a very strong Chair, and I clear it with him. But I would not talk to him without it being a step toward talking with the board about it. So I don't get very far without getting the board behind me.

This president says that he makes a point of maintaining social relationships with his trustees in order to stay "in favor."

A female executive director discussed her approach with the board. While it is similar to that of other CEOs, she spends more time politicking with the entire board, rather than just the Chair. She commented:

Before taking proposals to the board I have an idea on how each one of them is going to vote on each proposal. If I feel that it is a shaky vote, I will meet with the individual board members where I feel that there may be a problem. I may have them come to meetings of the organization in order to sell them so that when we have the board meeting I can get my vote.

Politics are a facet of almost any work situation, and although foundation staff were somewhat wary about discussing them with us, they almost all talked about the negotiating and "testing of the waters" with the board. But there is evidently wide variation in styles of negotiation.

Foundation Models

The balance between foundation board and staff roles ranges from situations where trustees run most aspects of grantmaking programs to those where employees have almost complete control. Along this continuum are what might be called the administrator model, director model, and presidential model.

In the administrator model, trustees are clearly dominant in the grants decision-making process. They are sometimes involved in the day-to-day operation of the foundation. Assets are limited, and staff size small, often only one or two persons. The program is most often directly related to the wishes of the donor. The CEO usually does not have the title of either president or executive director. Employees organize the foundation routine and provide materials to the board. Trustees discuss all proposals and make all funding decisions.

In the director model, the operating style is generally collegial. The CEO, usually an executive director, consults often with trustees about the grantmaking program and policies. This model primarily occurs in middle-sized to large foundations that may still have some donor or family participation. Trustees discuss recommended grant proposals, vote on funding, and decide on fiscal and grant program policies.

The presidential model is usually found in larger foundations that no longer have significant donor influence. Trustees delegate wide authority to the chief staff officer, who normally holds the title of president. The CEO provides leadership to foundation employees and the board. Trustees set fiscal and program policies, monitor progress, and make decisions on only very large grant proposals. Usually their CEO is someone nationally prominent, powerful, or well-respected in his own right.

Obviously these are models, and actual foundations mix characteristics from each. The incentives for the board to delegate more authority to the executive of a large foundation where hundreds of grants are made each year are obvious. In family-oriented foundations, trustees who knew the donor may feel an obligation to maintain the charitable directions established by that person.

Board Meeting Attendance

All CEOs regularly attend board meetings. Those who are trustees have a vote. In the interview sample, eleven (seven men and four women) of the 27 CEOs serve on the board. Presidents of foundations with over $25 million in assets and CEOs of corporate foundations often serve as full members of the board of trustees or distribution committee of their organizations. The president of a relatively new foundation described his rationale for wanting to be a board member:

> I also have a vote on the board. There are twenty-five foundations who do it, and the best foundations do. There are times when you have to address your trustees not as an employee, but as a fellow trustee. There are all kinds of issues in which it just makes it easier.

Some CEOs who are also board members had been trustees of the foundation prior to their appointment as president. Others said that they had insisted on board membership as a condition of employment. One president mentioned that his predecessor had been a trustee of the foundation, but he was of another opinion, and said: "I refused that when it was offered. I don't believe in staff becoming board members."

John W. Nason, an expert on foundation trusteeship, noted recently:

> The question is sometimes raised whether the professional head of a foundation should be a trustee of the foundation. In my judgment it does not make any difference whichever way this is settled. An effective chief executive officer will be just as influential reporting to a board of which he or she is not a member as to one on which he or she sits. In theory the employees of the board should not sit on the board; in practice it makes little difference. [Nason 1977; reported in Odendahl and Boris 1983a, p. 41]

However, CEOs who are also board members are widely perceived to have greater authority than their nontrustee counterparts.

Program officers and administrative assistants help prepare board materials, usually called "dockets" in the foundation field. Program officers write summaries of projects they have reviewed and include funding recommendations for the board. Some administrative assistants actually prepare the docket books; at the very least they make sure that all the supporting documents are in order. They are sometimes asked to take notes at board meetings; unless this is expected, administrative assistants are usually not allowed to attend. However, administrative assistants are often responsible for meeting arrangements. They also usually prepare and distribute any minutes and other reports after the board meeting.

Over half of the program officers we interviewed do not attend board meetings unless they are asked to make special presentations. A program officer characterized the typical situation: "I don't usually attend. If my director feels comfortable with the topic, I'm not invited to go. It keeps the board room from looking full." It also restricts lines of communication to trustees and keeps power centralized in the hands of the CEO.

Nine program officers in the sample report that they regularly attend board meetings, but their roles vary. One program officer said that he explains the nature of the projects and the rationale for his recommendations, but does not take part in any discussion. But another, who participates in the full meeting, commented: "We do the actual presentations, and we defend, and we interact with the board, as the staff responsible for that particular grant." The following description by another program officer illustrates how her attendance at board meetings increases her access to information and enriches her job situation:

> Our board is a fairly active board. They are not a rubber stamp. My sense is that at other foundations it's pretty much pro forma that everything goes through. On the other hand, it's very rare that something does not go through once it's brought to the board. There is quite a bit of substantive discussion of the merits of each proposal. We can count on the fact that unless we're very pressed for time, every proposal is going to get a full discussion.

Most program officers who are not allowed to attend board meetings wish that they could and view this restriction as a limitation on their authority. One program officer explained: "When I was hired I insisted that I had to come to the board meetings, because I wasn't expected to."

Program Evaluation and Policymaking

Although long-range planning is normally considered the responsibility of the board and the chief executive, five of the program officers we interviewed also mentioned it as one of their duties. In two cases, planning is a sizable portion of the job. Such long-range planning involves an evaluation component as well. Some foundations evaluate their various program areas every few years. This strategy often requires position papers from staff members in particular areas. One program officer explained the procedure at his foundation:

> Every few years staff presents general papers to the board with suggestions for future activities. The board discusses that with staff, and then some decisions are reached about the overall guidelines. Beyond that, every so often the board takes even more initiative. A committee is formed to look at the overall activities of the foundation, for the next decade or so. They meet on their own, and then they meet with staff.

Staff members, or program officers under the direction of the chief executive, produce the research necessary for a decision on long-range planning by the board of trustees. But the ongoing daily workload keeps many foundation employees from focusing on planning for the future.

Foundation staff members serve the board, but employees indicate that they have significant influence in the grantmaking and policy-setting process. Although staff members administer foundation programs on the basis of priorities set by trustees, they often emphasize that in practice criteria and guidelines can be both developed and implemented by employees. Understandably, in the interview situation, staff may be inclined to aggrandize their position, stressing those aspects of their work that show them guiding or even directing policy. Executives may also, of course, have reason to minimize their directiveness, depending upon their notion of the appropriate management model. The general impression received from discussion of board-staff relations is that men CEOs are more likely to stress their power with the board; women CEOs stress their efforts implementing and politicking to accomplish their work. Both men and women, program officers and administrative assistants, focus on their dependence upon the pleasure of the CEO for any relations with the board.

Women and Men in the Hierarchy

The foundation field is bifurcated, with the 30 to 40 heavily endowed, highly staffed foundations providing a more structured workplace and better compensation than the nearly 1,500 staffed foundations with smaller endowments and only a few employees. Foundations with over $100 million in assets employ over half of the full-time professional employees in the 1982 *CB Survey* sample. Two thirds of those professionals are men. This pattern is in contrast to foundations with less than $100 million in assets, where 54 percent of professionals are women.

Salaries[3]

While average salaries compare favorably with those of other occupations (see Table 4), men hold most of the highly compensated CEO positions. The median salary for female chief executives is $30,100, while for males it is $51,900, a ratio of 0.58. Among program officers, the median salary for women is $29,800, compared with $45,000 for men, a ratio of 0.66. These salary differentials are significantly related to the structure of the foundation field and to the personal characteristics of the staff members. Yet even when both structural and individual factors are taken into consideration, female gender is associated with lower salaries.

Female CEOs head only two of the 36 foundations in the *CB Survey* sample with more than $100 million in assets, or the equivalent in grantmaking. In foundations with less than $100 million in assets, almost one third of the 149 executives are women.

The average salary for CEOs from the largest foundations is almost three times that of executives from the smallest foundations. Female CEOs are clustered in small foundations, and this accounts for some of the observed difference in the compensation of male and female executives. But female CEOs also

---

[3] See statistical appendix for detailed methodology and analysis.

Table 4. Comparisons of Average Foundation Professional and Academic Salaries with Similar Groups of Workers (1981–82)

Annual Earnings	Panel 1 Federal Government	Panel 2 Private Industry	Panel 3 Broad Occupational Groups	Panel 4 Professional and Managerial Occupations	Panel 5 Higher Education Faculty	Panel 6 Foundation Professional
$80,000						
$70,000		$76,200 (Attorneys)				
$60,000		$62,490 (Engineers) $61,260				
$50,000	$53,510 (GS-15)					$56,430 (CEOs)
$40,000		$40,210 (Chemists)		$46,530 (Self-employed Physicians and Dentists)		$42,600 (Other Professionals) $39,400 (Program Officers)
	·$38,570 (GS-13)			$38,500 (Salaried Physicians and Dentists)		
		$33,410 (Buyers) $31,660 (Accountants) $31,220 (Job Analysts)			$33,480 (Full Professors)	
$30,000						
	$26,590 (GS-11)			$27,880 (Other Self-employed Professionals) $27,430 (College Professors) $26,660 (Salaried Managers)		
			$25,650 (Professionals) $25,430 (Managers)		$25,750 (All Ranks)	
					$25,210 (Associate Professors)	
		$22,330 (Sales)			$20,630 (Assistant Professors)	
$20,000		$20,260 (All Workers) $20,100 (Craft)				
					$16,310 (Instructors)	

SOURCES: American Association of University Professors 1983; Boris and Hooper 1982.

17

have lower salaries than their male colleagues who work at grantmaking institutions of similar size.

The wage gap for women program officers is 66.5 cents for every dollar earned by men, almost 10 percent higher than the ratio for male and female CEO salaries. Gender explains a greater proportion of the salary differential between male and female program officers than do other variables. Asset or equivalent grant level is the next most important determinant of salary levels for program officers. Female program officers are more likely to be employed by smaller foundations than their male counterparts, but over half of them work in the largest foundations. In large grantmaking organizations that have several levels of program positions, women are more likely to be employed in the middle and lower levels than are men. Only 13 percent of the 163 men who are program officers earn salaries of less than $30,000, while 56 percent of the 158 women have salaries in that range.

An examination of compensation data for other foundation executive and professional positions reveals that there is also a substantial salary differential between men and women in these jobs. Once again, a greater proportion of men (79 percent) work in the higher-paying large foundations, while women are almost equally divided between large and small foundations. In addition, women occupy more of the lower-level professional positions, while men hold most of the high-paying vice-presidential and officer jobs. On the average, women are paid less even when they occupy similar positions.

While part of this pattern results from the hiring of women for newly created positions as staffing in the field has expanded, it also reflects institutional discrimination and societal norms that assign women to lower-level and less prestigious positions. Women are more likely to be hired as office managers than as vice-presidents for administration. Their salary levels are correspondingly lower, ranging from 63 to 69 percent of male income depending on the size of the foundation.

For women, the structure of opportunity is clearly greater in small foundations and in positions below that of CEO. An executive position is accessible to women almost exclusively in small foundations. But, in many cases, the CEO job in such grantmaking institutions does not carry the degree of prestige or the complexity of managerial responsibility that it does in larger foundations. Compared with men who are executives, a smaller proportion of women have trustee status or serve with the most prestigious titles.

Titles and Trusteeship

President and executive director are the titles most frequently reported by CEOs. Those at the largest foundations have the title of president, whereas at the smaller grantmaking organizations there are an equal number of presidents and executive directors. Virtually all private foundations with asset levels of over $100 million employ men as CEOs and use the title president. There are few presidents, male or female, in foundations with less than $10 million in assets. Two thirds of the male CEOs in the interview sample hold the title of president; only one third of the female executives are presidents. Far more female than male CEOs are assigned other titles, such as administrator.

Women executives are increasingly aware of the distinctions that a title may carry. One woman had made an unsuccessful attempt to change her title and was looking for a new position as a consequence. But another had managed to lobby with her board for a change in title:

> I finally said to the board, "In my position, I am doing things that are very similar to colleagues in the field who have the title of executive director. I have been with this organization for a fairly long time, and this is the top administrative job in the foundation. I feel that a job title would at least give me some sense that I was proceeding along some kind of career ladder, and also put me on a more even keel with titles that are more common within the field."

Women in the sample tend to believe that it is important to work with at least the title of executive director. This belief may be an indication of both career and gender-equity consciousness developing among women in the field.

Another status distinction between male and female foundation CEOs concerns trusteeship. Presidents of large foundations are most likely to serve as voting members of the board of directors. Few female CEOs have such status. The importance attached to serving as a trustee was illustrated by one of our respondents. Her title had been upgraded, but she thought of the "promotion" as a device to get her off the board, where she had served for a number of years. She said: "I was made CEO partly as an honor, but it was one of those honors that kill you, because the board attached a provision that the CEO could not be a member. In a sense, it has been a loss of power, a restraint." This is a unique situation in which a trade-off between a prestigious title and trusteeship was required. It is clear in this case that board status is the more important factor in running the foundation.

Management

Chief executive officers are responsible for the hiring and firing of foundation employees, delegating tasks, and direct supervision, or the establishing of reporting relationships. Some of the largest foundations have personnel departments, but most grantmaking institutions are so small that CEOs manage staffing directly. A few administrative assistants are also involved with personnel matters. One explained:

> I keep attendance records. I deal with people on the phone looking for employment, and I answer all the letters requesting employment. I work with people on their vacations, and keep track of that status for each person, personal and sick leave and coordinating people's time out of the office.

19

Program officers, sometimes called program directors at larger foundations, may also have hiring and supervisory duties. Most often in their interviews, however, CEOs referred to the responsibility for staffing and management. As one executive commented: "I love the people I work with, whom I chose."

Management styles vary. A CEO with a fairly large staff described his role:

> The political management of the enterprise, the integrating of things, the providing of basic direction, a sense of pace, values, communication of vision, engendering of a sense of shared purpose, the creation of a working environment that's productive, and innovative, and fun.

A president spoke of his management style:

> We have a very democratic approach to administration. I don't believe in autocratic administration. I believe in giving people a lot of latitude and a lot of freedom to be creative, but to understand the dynamics and the framework in which we operate, and expect them to demonstrate good judgment within that.

Some CEOs indicated that they had worked under tyrants, although none described themselves as autocrats. One had been so negatively affected by his first foundation boss that he made sure his management style was nearly the opposite. He explained:

> I was taught under the old style of foundation administration. Proposals would come into my boss's office once a week. He would have them stacked up and he would go through them. He would say, "Here is a proposal from the University of ———. I've worked with them in the past. I think that's excellent. We have a proposal here from XYZ organization. It's just crap. I don't know these fuzzy-headed liberals. I don't think you should spend much time on this thing." And so on. When I left that meeting, I knew rather precisely what I ought to do about every project that was in front of me. If I wanted to go against something that he was for, I had a major battle on my hands. It was not so much an intellectual challenge as it was a political challenge, and he had all the votes.

Another foundation president was probably candid in his description of his management style:

> It is much closer to consensual, with occasional bursts of hierarchical decisions. We have a really anomalous, pervasive collegial approach. Ideas originate in a number of places. It might be a blind request. It might be something that came from a discussion between the president and another member of the staff, or with an individual who somehow stimulates an idea. Everything that is eventually presented to the board for recommendation is

discussed in both substantive and also editorial detail by the entire staff. Every now and then I exert my magnificent and omnipotent power. Sometimes, for example, there is a very strong board interest in a proposal and there isn't any point in pretending that that isn't going to come up to the board. That is not so much authoritative as it is a practical matter. If I'm not persuaded about the damn proposal, it is not going to go, and everybody knows it.

Some of the power that a CEO exerts over subordinates can be couched in terms of board policy, especially in those instances where other staff members do not attend board meetings. The management approaches of both women and men are diverse. However, many women do not have other staff members reporting to them, and if they do, they say they use more conciliatory management strategy than men. While the style may be collegial, the underlying structure of authority resembles the traditional hierarchical arrangement in modern office bureaucracy.

Corporate foundations are usually more bureaucratic than other foundation types, as they are normally subsumed within the hierarchy of a large company that provides funds for grantmaking. The company CEO's policy and style have an impact on foundation operation. An executive at a corporate foundation may report directly to the company president or to a vice-president within the firm. Occasionally the CEO of the foundation is a vice-president, although these individuals generally have other responsibilities in the company as well, and most delegate the foundation work to subordinates. A few corporate foundations have autonomy from their mother company, but this is not the rule.

In the same vein, many "independent" foundations actually operate out of the business office of the donor or family and are thus closer to the corporate form. Corporate foundation workplaces tend to be formal and involve strict compliance with company rules. Most community and independent foundations have informal organizational arrangements. Staff size varies, but size, in combination with asset or grant level, has the greatest bearing on the complexity of reporting relationships and exercise of authority. Obviously, larger grantmaking institutions tend to be more bureaucratic than smaller ones. More variation in management style is found in small and medium-sized family and community foundations where flexibility and informality are possible.

The individual preferences and personalities of CEOs contribute to diversity in foundation jobs and workplaces. One administrative assistant explained: "The quality of the people in top management is most important in making this a pleasant place to work with high morale."

CEOs we interviewed characterized their relationships with staff as "friendly and trusting," although some program officers and administrative assistants disagreed with this characterization. Presidents and executive directors have power over other foundation employees because they can always veto their subordinates' recommendations. In certain foundations, program officers or administrative assistants do the research and technical work in preparation for an executive's decision and presentation to the board or distribution committee. A few program officers object to what they consider the arbitrary decisions of their bosses. In contrast, a consensual proposal review process was described by the president of a foundation with several staff members: "We do it all together. We see each other every day, and every application that comes in is read by all of us. We all comment, and we get together and decide what to do with it." Most executives say they operate with a "collegial" or egalitarian management style, but they still have authority over other employees, and are accountable to a board of trustees.

Financial Duties

Financial responsibilities usually distinguish the CEO from other foundation positions. Such financial matters include budget preparation, distribution of any discretionary funds, and sometimes managing or overseeing investments. Fiscal duties are considered quite important in the foundation field as elsewhere because the control of money is associated with power.

At many grantmaking organizations budgeting is informal and based largely on estimates of interest income and the previous year's expenditures. A few foundations develop a budget that serves as a policy instrument for the coming year. Sophisticated financial practices are being adopted in the foundation community as the connection between the policies of an organization and its budget are better understood. But even with clear-cut administrative and giving criteria, an attempt is often made to build flexibility into a budget. Several foundations allocate specific sums to their major funding or program areas and reserve a certain amount for innovative projects. CEOs and program directors must balance the need for formalized planning with a capability to seize opportunities for creative grantmaking.

The budgets of many foundations include "presidential" discretionary funds earmarked for emergency situations, small grants, special programs, or creative ventures. Decisions about these funds are usually the prerogative of the chief executive, or sometimes vice-presidents or program directors at larger foundations. While discretionary funds have been criticized because of the possibility of abuse, they also allow for prompter emergency grantmaking as well as greater independence and latitude on the part of foundation staff. Nine of the foundation CEOs we interviewed referred to discretionary funds at their organizations. These funds range from $10,000 to $850,000, with $2,000 to $100,000 grant restrictions to any one organization.

Discretionary funds are not always desired. A president at one of the largest foundations put it this way: "No. Don't use it; don't want it." But another said:

I have a presidential slush fund, staff grant fund, or whatever you want to call it, which isn't very much. But we try to use it as wisely as we can. I can get more if I want from the board. I just don't want any more than that. But rather than use that for gifts to friends—well, I'm not saying that a lot of people do it, but I don't want to do it—we're using that as sort of start-up funds for things that are quite different, where somebody needs money to see if something's going to work or not.

All but one of the individuals we interviewed who control discretionary funds are also on the board of trustees at their foundations. Only one woman CEO mentioned such a fund, with the lowest dollar limit in the sample. Discretionary funds and trusteeship are clear indicators of authority in grantmaking organizations, and they are more prevalent at large foundations and those with male chief executives.

Although executives normally make final decisions or recommendations to the board about the use of foundation funds, other employees keep track of the expenditures. In some foundations administrative assistants are doing work which would be delegated to professional staff or even CEOs in other organizations. A few administrative assistants monitor grant applications and money expended by the foundation. One administrative assistant, who is primarily responsible for such activities, explained:

I follow all the routine from the office point of view: procedures for collecting information, for making grants, getting grants approved, for payments, and then filing, making sure that the reporting is complete. I have to work with the secretary of the foundation in terms of expenditure responsibility, which is a classification of certain grants by the tax laws. He makes a report every year to the IRS, and I have to supply him with all the information for that report.

When asked about her job duties, another administrative assistant commented: "Reports are the most important—investment updates, conflict of interest reports. A big part is preparing our book [docket] for the board meeting, and our treasurer's report." Another keeps track of the status of the budget as part of her job. She said: "I do the financial statements. I develop all the reports so that decisions can be made."

Administrative Support Staff

All the administrative assistants in the sample are designated "support" staff in their foundations, in contrast to "professional" staff members such as CEOs and program officers. The designation of support seems satisfactory to the employees themselves. An administrative assistant commented: "I like a fairly structured situation. I really don't want to be involved in decision-making." Even those administrative assistants with supervisory responsibilities do not see their jobs as leadership positions, but rather as auxiliary to their bosses'. This distinction between clerical and other foundation jobs is evident in the descriptions they gave of their duties, and it shows in the self-images of the administrative assistants we interviewed as well.

At the beginning of her interview, one administrative assistant said: "I honestly don't know too much." When asked how her position fit into the overall personnel structure she commented: "They call me support staff." However, she clearly described the programs of the foundation and the complexity of her job responsibilities, many of which fall into the "professional" category. She indicated that her lack of ambition is tied to her status as a clerical worker. "I was always content with being a secretary. I never really got into worrying about wanting to get further. It was not part of my pattern." Another administrative assistant consistently referred to the "girls" and the "men" in the office. These girls are all clerical workers, in comparison to the "professional" men. One administrative assistant said that she enjoys her job and thinks that she has been extremely lucky: "I have had the opportunity to work with what I would say are the top men in the country. I really mean that. I just consider myself most fortunate."

In some cases, the administrative assistants' perception of their work is mirrored by their bosses. As one administrative assistant explained: "I know at one time our administrative officer wanted me to write a job description and my boss said: 'Forget it. She's just an extension of me.'" Several indicated that their jobs involve doing whatever their bosses ask of them, that they cannot control their own time because they are at the beck and call of their supervisors.

However, what administrative assistants actually do can range across professional as well as secretarial tasks. One writes press releases, monitors newspapers for stories on the foundation or its grantees, and maintains a clipping book. Another does editing. One manages the printing of the annual report, which includes preparing camera-ready artwork. Another acts as librarian: selecting, ordering, and organizing all foundation books, journals, and resource materials. But these opportunities for administrative assistants are found in the smaller foundations where the hierarchy is not as rigidly structured. The relative scarcity of administrative assistants in the larger foundations suggests that the duties of support staff are limited to secretarial-clerical tasks; the discretionary aspects of office routines are handled by program assistants and associates.

Most administrative assistants enjoy their work, but some have a sense of isolation because of their employment in the foundation field. They see themselves as envied by other office workers and beleaguered by grant applicants. One of them said: "No one really is your friend. Everybody wants your job. It's a very rough job, because everybody is calling and writing for money."

Job Satisfaction

Satisfaction with one's work relates to position in a hierarchy. CEOs, with the most authority and prestige of all foundation employees, are the most satisfied. CEOs have high status in the community and often nationally. Foundation executives feel they have almost unlimited access to ideas, information, and people, as well as the opportunity to have a real impact on their program areas. One president commented: "The flexibility is vast. The work is interesting. We are able to have some effect. I feel potent. I feel the institution is effective. I enjoy what I think is a generally good, I believe, deserved reputation for doing pretty good work."

Chief executives of grantmaking organizations exercise authority and discretion on an almost daily basis. Although they report to a board of directors, they administer substantial sums of money, and their funding recommendations generally carry great weight. Foundation executives have both freedom and influence in the nonprofit arena. The president of a large grantmaking institution told us: "I don't know that I've ever dreaded coming to work. There are days when I sort of resent some of the impositions. But I love the flexibility. You're always challenged and intrigued by a new idea, [or] the people you come in contact with." One director said: "There are very few things about this job that I don't enjoy. It's about as close to being a fully satisfying job as I can imagine."

Program officers also report high job satisfaction, but they are not as overwhelmingly pleased with their work situations as the CEOs. Most of the program officers we interviewed said they liked "the opportunity to have contact with all kinds of people. We all enjoy that the most. There has never been a boring day. You are always seeing different organizations and hearing from different people." But program officers have less authority and control over their activities than CEOs and often need clearance to pursue special interests. When asked what she liked least about her job, one program officer commented: "the dictatorial nature of our set-up." Another indicated:

> If you are a dynamic and a free thinker, the profession does not support you. I have not been terribly impressed by the quality of the people I've met, with some exceptions. There are real limitations in the kinds of people who sit on boards. I don't think that they are necessarily qualified for the positions they have.

These negative statements may reflect a perceived lack of opportunity for nonexecutives in the foundation community. Rosabeth Moss Kanter (1977a) has argued that when structural work arrangements place individuals in low opportunity positions they tend to "be critical of high-powered people, of management, or at least fail to identify with them" (p. 247). On the other hand, several program officers do identify with their supervisors and board members and aspire to upper management positions at foundations.

Program officers expressed a greater degree of frustration than CEOs, although the issues were the same. Program officers do more of the declination work; one commented on what she least likes: "Having to say no. Doubting your values and priorities as the basis for saying no. It creates a lot of self-doubt." Several mentioned their desire to be closer to the action in which grantees are involved. As a program officer said:

> It gets to be very frustrating in that you are always dealing in a superficial way with important things that people are doing, and you are never really involved. And you are never on a really person-to-person basis, because always you are the funder, and they are always guarding themselves.

Employees of grantmaking organizations face conflicts regarding how friendly they can be with grantseekers to whom they may eventually say no. In addition, most foundation staff are not "in the works," running programs they think are important. Like their bosses, program officers juggle a variety of activities. Most are enthusiastic about their jobs and report innovative approaches to their work. But program officers have less autonomy than chief executive officers, and while they usually make funding recommendations, they can be overruled.

Administrative assistants in the sample like their jobs, but they expect less from them than other foundation employees. Only one administrative assistant spoke of career aspirations or of the possibility of moving out of the clerical area into program work at the foundation. Most of them feel fortunate to be associated with people they admire and seem to derive their job satisfaction from the work of the foundation or their bosses, rather than their own activities. Two administrative assistants made altruistic statements about their work. One said: "I like the idea of assistance for people to help themselves." Another commented: "It's an interesting field, and it is rewarding. In some small way you feel that you are doing your part for mankind. Whereas in industry you don't have that good feeling."

When asked what they liked best about their jobs, one of the administrative assistants said: "I like the whole thing." Another replied: "I like the physical surrounding and then the liberal benefits." One administrative assistant explained: "It lets me do pretty much what I am interested in. I do have free time, and that free time can be used toward volunteer work for nonprofits." Most of them said they enjoyed "the people, the relationships, and the atmosphere."

When asked what she enjoys least about her work an administrative assistant said: "the tedium." Another firmly replied: "filing." But these dissatisfactions, as well as the advantages that are appreciated, are consequences of where administrative assistants find themselves in the hierarchy of management.

Summary

The overall impression garnered from interviews is that foundations provide a congenial pocket of employment in a world where working conditions are not usually so satisfactory. CEOs have wide opportunity to exercise discretion and display personal style as they engage in policy planning and creative grantmaking, and participate in community or even national affairs. Opportunities for women to become executives are greatest in foundations with assets of less than $100 million or the equivalent in grantmaking or program activities; but the salary levels in these foundations are lower than in the largest foundations. Program officers may suffer or profit from the benign paternalism of the CEO; but they have avenues for the exercise of professional skills and access to networks that can help in improving them. However, female program officers earn substantially less than their male counterparts. Support staff are grateful to find themselves in this congenial pocket, in comparison with other worlds of secretarial-clerical employment.

3

The Daily Work of Foundation Employees

Foundations range from post office boxes and one-person shops to a few institutions with several hundred employees. About 6,000 people work at staffed foundations across the country. These grantmaking organizations account for more than half the field's $48 billion in assets.

Many foundations occupy well-appointed suites in modern skyscrapers. Others operate from corporate headquarters or in buildings owned by the grantmaking organization. A few are housed in unpretentious single rooms. Foundation offices are in cities, suburbs, and rural areas, although almost one third of the country's grantmaking organizations are in New York. The resources of a foundation usually determine the number of staff members, as well as the size and nature of office space. Private grantmaking organizations generally have fewer than five employees.

There is a world of difference between the operation of a small foundation with one paid staff person who gives away $500,000 a year and that of a large grantmaking organization such as The Ford Foundation with over 340 employees and annual grants of $85 million. The Ford Foundation has its own building in New York City and programs with national and international impact. It has a complex internal bureaucracy. In contrast, small family foundations usually distribute their funds in a local community and are managed informally without personnel policies or salary scales.

Foundation work involves a curious mixture of altruism and arrogance. The ideology of philanthropy is that grantmakers wish to improve the general well-being of society, but hope to remain selfless and humble about these efforts. A foundation president explained:

The only thing that really counts is doing some good in the world. You're not trying to make a profit. You're not trying to win a championship. You're not trying to do anything but make a difference on the right side. I think that can be a very comforting circumstance, provided that you don't get smug and complacent.

But this posture of selflessness and humility is always threatened. Another foundation employee remarked: "People sitting on a big pile of money get very pleased with themselves." The nature of the work contributes to this situation. Staff members at grantmaking institutions report that they feel isolated and must exercise caution in developing friendships with grantseekers who are often ingratiating because they are competing for scarce resources. One foundation employee said that after he obtained his job: "I had my last bad meal. I lost my last true friend. And, I heard my last honest compliment."

General Office Routine

Grantmaking is the central business of foundations, but some staff members stressed this aspect of their work more than others. For example, the job duties many executives perform are primarily administrative. A president of a large foundation explained:

> I am responsible for the administration of the place. It follows that I have those responsibilities any chief executive has: the performance of the people who report to me, and the people who report to them; keeping the finances straight, not spending more than we are supposed to, or notably less. No appropriation goes to the board without my supporting it. I think beyond that, I am expected to be a critical person.

CEOs in the largest foundations spend more time in administration than in direct proposal review, which is the responsibility of program officers who report to them. Executives of smaller foundations are usually more involved with investigating grant applications and monitoring projects, although they also depend on other staff members such as administrative assistants.

Most foundations are inundated with requests for information and money. Telephones ring continually, and mail is copious. A foundation president commented on the office routine:

> It is a question of just organizing the deluge of material. My office has sometimes as many as eighty phone calls [a day]. We keep a roster, and if I go away for several days, that is death to the list. It's a process of incoming calls and outgoing ones. And I have anywhere between twenty and fifty letters a day.

This press of work is mediated for professionals by their support staff. Although CEOs and program officers referred to their direction of the daily office work, clerical staff members actually undertake most of it.

Administrative assistants must have substantial understanding of program priorities, for they are often the first foundation employees who respond to grantseekers and their proposals. An administrative assistant at a large foundation explained:

> I keep track of all the requests that come in, and the various stages of progression. I send out letters reminding grantees about reports that are due. We have turn-down letters for the bulk of the requests that come in. I'm the one that sort of assigns which letter goes to whom. I follow up if there are questions about turn-down letters and about grants.

Those remarks suggest that in addition to logging proposals, some administrative assistants have the authority to decline applications clearly outside the giving criteria of the foundation. They check to see that proposals are complete, and in some cases, without further guidance from the CEO, they route them to the appropriate program officer for review and recommendation. If funding has been authorized, administrative assistants may monitor the financial and record-keeping aspects of foundation grants as well.

Many administrative assistants serve as office managers. At large foundations they supervise the clerical staff; in smaller grantmaking organizations administrative assistants are responsible for all the clerical tasks. They develop office systems, keep the files organized, and make sure that supplies are in order and stocked. Administrative assistants often coordinate foundation conferences and meetings. They maintain office equipment and arrange for service contracts. Most administrative assistants "play it by ear" as a matter of course in their work. They do whatever needs to be done. Their work ranges from what might normally be considered professional to providing personal services for their bosses. For example, several have accounting and bookkeeping responsibilities, but they also water the office plants and make the morning coffee.

An administrative assistant may act as an executive secretary or work for several foundation staff members. She "protects" chief executives and program officers from interruptions by screening telephone calls and visitors. Many administrative assistants keep their bosses' calendars, make their appointments, and see to travel arrangements. They generally keep the foundation organized, and facilitate the work of other staff members.

Correspondence

Correspondence consumes a great deal of foundation employees' time. Both program officers and administrative assistants have varying amounts of authority for correspondence. According to a program officer:

> Probably eighty percent of the foundation's correspondence goes out under a program officer's signature. A lot of the stuff that comes addressed to the president will go out under a program officer's signature. The responsive aspects of the job are more routine, and the least attractive are the decline letters. I have written and told people their proposal needed some editing to make it persuasive. Some things like that give you a chance to contribute.

These remarks suggest that declining applications and proposals is onerous work and that program officers are largely responsible for it. But program officers emphasize their advisory and consulting capacities in suggestions they can offer to make projects better. This is a way to make the onerous correspondence more interesting.

Administrative assistants are generally responsible for routine correspondence; however, many also have a fair amount of discretion, although they rarely receive recognition for this work. Most administrative assistants type their bosses' letters. Many of them also draft and write responses to grant applications and requests for additional materials. In these cases, a program officer or CEO usually signs the document. An administrative assistant commented: "I don't sign the declination myself. The program officer approves the responses that I do, signs the correspondence, and becomes familiar with each and every applicant's request." One assistant saw most of her work as routine:

> I take care of report reminders and stuff like that. "Please send us a copy of your IRS letter." I handle that. The CEO, because he does all the program work, does all the denials and various things like that. When it comes time for the granting, all those people who do receive grants get a standard grant letter. The CEO gives me all the information, and I plug it in and send it out.

But another talked about areas of discretion in her work: "I do a lot of drafting of correspondence. We have a great many letters that we're not able to respond to favorably, and I do a lot of that." Although the correspondence that administrative assistants handle is generally fairly routine, it often requires judgment. If an application is not declined outright, it is usually referred to a program officer or executive for review.

Proposal Review

During her interview, a program officer provided a description of her standard job duties: "I think the initial responsibility is screening inquiries and investigating an inquiry, perhaps turning that inquiry into a full-fledged application. Also, site visits of applicants, preparing a review of applications, and recommendations to the board." An inquiry may be a written request for funding or a telephone call soliciting information. Most program officers have the authority to make a decision at any number of points about whether or not to proceed with an inquiry. If it does not fit within the criteria or guidelines of the foundation, the proposal is usually declined. The decision on such a declination is often made by a program officer, if not already made by either an administrative assistant or the chief executive. CEOs generally know about declinations because rejection letters often go out under their signatures.

CEOs may exercise their authority or delegate it. In most grantmaking organizations the CEO determines who will review applications on any given topic, although, as noted, administrative assistants sometimes route proposals to program officers who are expected to manage specific funding areas. In ten of the 42 foundations in the sample, the entire program staff, including the CEO, review all the inquiries that fall within grantmaking guidelines. A program officer talked about this procedure: "We sit down with the inquiries that we think should go to full-fledged applications, and talk about them. It is more or less, 'I'll look into that.' 'Do you want to look into that?' It is very free-flowing."

Some proposals are rejected after deliberations at staff meetings. Others are divided among the program staff for further work, in preparation for a recommendation to the board. If a proposal or suggested project idea seems worthwhile, a program officer or CEO begins investigating the submitting organization. At some foundations the program officer needs the approval of the president or executive director before proceeding.

Any number of activities might take place next, depending on the style of the CEO or program officer and the tradition of the foundation. The proposal might be sent for peer review to a committee of specialists or consultants with expertise in a program area. In these cases foundation employees must recruit readers and sometimes organize meetings to consider recommendations.

In addition, a site visit may be arranged, or key staff members from the applying organization may be invited for a discussion at the foundation's offices. Staff members usually do research on the organization prior to such a meeting. They might call colleagues at other foundations to see if they have ever funded or even heard of the organization. Agencies that handle programs similar to the applicant's may be asked about the reputation of the grantseeker. After review of submitted materials, additional information might also be requested.

Even if program officers or executives always review proposals in a specific area, they must be generalists as well. This requirement is especially likely at small foundations. One program officer said:

> I have the primary responsibility here for the health work that we do. I do a fair amount of grants review and work in higher education and a fair amount in human services. It is the character of this place that each of the program officers has one area to shepherd, and then what is in everybody else's area as well. So it's a collegial pattern.

Although a staff member is often familiar with a particular field, it is impossible for that person to understand fully all the ramifications of a specific project without extensive investigation. In addition to the substantive portions of the proposal, foundation employees must also consider the budget and the ability of the applicant to complete the project. Of course, a staff member may review hundreds of applications, and so some receive more thorough examination and investigation than others.

Brokering

Brokering is a significant activity of some foundation employees, primarily CEOs and program officers. They are often advocates for projects they endorse. An executive director at a medium-sized foundation explained brokering in this way: "Part of my job is to lever and to promote what we are funding. And it is an example of the politician aspect that is part and parcel of grantmaking." A staff member may solicit additional funding from other organizations for a grantee; convene a conference of individuals and groups working on similar issues; or arrange technical assistance for worthy, but needy, projects.

Technical assistance might involve guidance in any number of areas. Nonprofit organizations that receive foundation funds may not have the managerial expertise to ensure completion of their projects. According to foundation employees, such organizations may need help with budgeting, additional fundraising, marketing, writing, or even board and staff development. Foundations may supply such services directly or contract with outside consultants to do so.

One program officer at an independent foundation highlighted his technical assistance activities. He contended that the reviewing, scrutinizing, and recommending of grants is the narrowest possible construction of his job. Wider community responsibilities are really paramount:

> I see the responsibility to be accessible to the nonprofit community, to provide in-kind or technical assistance to the community-based organizations to the extent that I can, whether or not we can grant to them. And I have a responsibility to be as well informed as I can on the characteristics of this community, and mediating between community-based organizations and nonprofits, and foundation-based staff. I think of myself as straddling the institutional setting where I work and the community. I don't feel as located within this institutional setting as some in the field might.

Some foundation officers are involved with developing and initiating projects. A program officer at a large foundation explained:

> We consider ourselves more entrepreneurial and activist than some foundation staff. We're not only reacting to proposals that come in, we are also working with grantees, and working with other foundations in designing activities. I think that this is consistent with creative philanthropy, and useful for small foundation activities.

Encouraging joint funding with other foundations is one of the methods that several staff members mentioned for increasing the impact of their work. Joint funding is sometimes initiated after one foundation has "discovered" or identified a particularly good project or group of people working on an idea. One grantmaker referred to these ventures as "investment banking":

> In due course we see that there are particularly good actors, particularly good ideas, and sometimes these are not presented to us. So we take the initiative and say, "Here's a need, or a gap." We either put together ideas or we ask someone else to put together ideas and we play a catalytic, entrepreneurial role. In these situations we are often playing an investment banker role, where we will look at the ideas that are presented to us on the basis of this active involvement in the subject. We will put our endorsement and some money up front and we will then try to get other money into the process.

Such a view of a foundation officer's responsibility suggests quite aggressive intervention in the programs of nonprofit organizations. Other foundations may not define their roles this way, or may be understaffed, and their employees are either too busy or do not have the expertise necessary to provide technical assistance. Staff members might like to be innovative and wish to initiate projects, but if this is not the normal style of the foundation they must solicit the approval of the CEO and board of trustees if they wish to do more than respond to proposals.

Networking

In addition to whatever brokering foundations do with one another and for community agencies they may fund, foundation employees are often expected to act as representatives of their grantmaking organizations by interacting with peers in the philanthropic community, attending social engagements, entertaining, and maintaining "visibility" with the public. Many of the employees we interviewed referred to these activities as "networking," a frequently used term.

The network concept is an abstraction developed by social scientists as a means of describing human interaction. A social network consists of a quasi-group of people who are connected to each other either through direct relationships or because of mutual acquaintances (Simmel 1955). In the foundation world and elsewhere, this abstraction has been applied to work situations. In this context, networking may involve attending local and national grantmaking conferences, meeting new people, and maintaining relationships in order to advance the foundation's projects or the staff member's career. For example, the more "contacts" that one has, the easier it is to ask for assistance on various projects—and to discover or be sponsored for better positions.

Many CEOs and program officers consider networking essential to their work because it provides a framework for the brokering and joint funding efforts that they see as an integral part of their jobs. Therefore, club and professional memberships are quite important. But more men than women in the interview sample have memberships that are paid for by the foundation. About three quarters of those who had foundation-paid memberships are men. Larger foundations are more likely to provide such perquisites. In smaller foundations, where there are fewer of these benefits, women are also less likely to receive them.

The kinds of networks that are accessible, and the desire to participate in them, vary with the status of individuals as well as their positions, for there are different levels of networking. Most of the foundation executives we interviewed said they spend considerable time interacting with peers. Several CEOs mentioned a prestigious foundation executives' group. One president said he appreciates:

> A foundation executives' group which is very informal and very quiet and doesn't take any actions, but meets once a year some place where we can sit down for two or three days and talk about our problems together. That's got about fifteen or sixteen people, not the fifteen or sixteen largest in order of endowment, but includes a good many of the major foundations.

Informal associations which foster networking are not always seen as desirable. The president of a large independent foundation gave his opinion:

> I think cooperation is a good thing but cartels are not. So I think that if you look at the foundation industry generally the criticism you would make of it is that it has in the past operated too much like a gentlemen's club. And so not forming many gentlemen's clubs in an urban area seems to me like a good idea. I talk quite a bit with other people about process, but we try and do our own homework, and reach our own independent judgments.

However, CEOs usually belong to at least one formal membership organization such as the Council on Foundations, a regional association, or groups that foster networking such as Women and Foundations/Corporate Philanthropy. (See Appendix 3.)

Program officers report networking activities less than CEOs. But those who are trying to establish careers in philanthropy or gain promotions in the foundation field see networking as essential. A program officer at a foundation funding research attends conferences and meetings in her professional area to keep up with the latest developments in the field. She said: "I try to keep up contact with people I know, and try to meet other people, to get a sense of what would be important to be doing in the field at the time."

Most program officers depend on organizations and colleagues in the philanthropic world. A program officer commented on the growing requirement for collaboration caused by economic exigencies: "With the way things are going in the economy, and the load of applicants, we all realize that we are going to have to combine our thoughts and rely on each other somewhat." In general, foundation employees rely on contacts in the field or experts they have cultivated over time to provide advice and consultation.

In addition to "substantive" networking, foundation CEOs are often expected to both host and attend social functions as part of their work. Such entertaining ranges from informal luncheons to elaborate banquets with community leaders, experts in their funding areas, grantees and potential grantees, and trustees. Cocktail receptions and dinner parties are common for some foundation executives. These events are often sponsored by grantees. More entertaining is required of chief executives in community and corporate foundations than in other grantmaking organizations. The head of a company-sponsored foundation attends social functions as a component of the job: "It requires that I attend them. We want the company image represented in the community. I don't have to give the parties myself. Frequently the company gives the party, but we want to be visible at important community functions and so I will go, even if it is boring."

Most CEOs at independent foundations perceive entertaining and social functions as a more limited aspect of their jobs. Other foundation executives are opposed to work-related social engagements. One president stated: "I say no to most social functions. They are an automatic no unless I am speaking. I just don't fool with that." A few are adamantly against being entertained, as is the following executive director: "Eight million people want to entertain us and we turn down ninety-nine point nine percent of the invitations. I don't like to do things at lunchtime because it stretches out so long. Usually I grab a sandwich with a colleague."

Only three foundation CEOs commented on the ethics of socializing with potential or current grantees. One president said:

> I insist that I pay my own way. It's an ethical question with me. I do not accept free box seats to the opera, free theater tickets. I never let anyone take me to lunch or dinner that I would talk to about a grant. I never allow a potential grantee to entertain me in any way. I feel very strongly about that.

An executive director thought that some social activities involve a conflict of interest:

> My policy, that the board adopted, though I don't think they approve of it very much, is that we don't take anything. We pay for tickets. I think the board humors me. My view is that it is a straight conflict of interest. And we want to show groups how to operate.

With regard to fundraising events, it is more complex. The thousand dollar dinner, we don't go to. If it is something that I think I should attend to show support, or that I might learn from it, or the foundation, and it's fifty or a hundred dollars a ticket, the foundation will buy tickets for me.

These remarks, offered spontaneously, suggest that ethics may be an emerging area of interest for those concerned with the professionalization of the field.[4]

Unlike CEOs, the program officers we interviewed are not required to attend foundation-related entertaining and social engagements, although many choose to participate. Those who report career aspirations are more likely to be involved with these activities. Some consider the program officer position a stepping-stone to a CEO or other high-level job and try to be more visible.

Foundation staff are frequently asked to give speeches or serve on panels at conferences. Some executives are interviewed by the press and make public statements, while others avoid exposure. Certain foundations have a policy of promoting their work. The CEOs of these organizations are frequently asked to make statements about projects they fund. The president of an activist grant-making organization explained:

> I make speeches. For some reason we're viewed as an expert in every area, and so we consider that very important, because it's a way to make people think, and to shape public opinion. We periodically do things to keep the issues in the public eye. This means that we are getting more and more sophisticated in marketing . . . a study means nothing unless people read it and understand the issue.

Visibility is a dimension of the job for many foundation CEOs and a few program officers. Program officers generally have little visibility, both locally and nationally, compared with foundation chief executives. Those who review applications in a particular community, or in a special funding area, may market their programs. One program officer commented:

> You don't have to be highly visible, but the more aggressive you are with ideas, the more you try to sell your ideas to other people—which is a little easier for foundations because they can back that sale up with a promise or at least the hope of some cash—the more visibility is required.

---

[4] The formulation of an ethical code is, after all, widely recognized as one effort by an aspiring occupation to become professional (Hughes 1958). *Foundation News*, the journal of the Council on Foundations, has been running a column on ethics since 1983, and all members of the Council are required to subscribe to a statement of principles and practices.

This desire for visibility varies from foundation to foundation and depends largely on policies of the board. Many grantmaking institutions prefer a low profile because they hope to limit the number of inquiries and proposals they receive.

Community and company-sponsored foundations often want good publicity so that their image is enhanced. Community foundations are anxious to increase bequests and contributions. The CEO of a community foundation explained:

> There are little gifts and there are big gifts: from estates, persons still living, corporations. Everything we do [is] visibly observed by donors. So our performance relates to fundraising. If we make lousy grants, that our donors don't like, most of them wouldn't say anything, they just wouldn't give us any more money.

Company-sponsored foundations operate with a slightly different approach, although public image is also a primary concern. The CEOs of major corporations view corporate giving as a "form of enlightened self-interest" (Yankelovich, Skelly and White 1982, p. 59). A corporate officer is often more visible than the foundation administrator. The issue is not who gets publicity, but how it is best obtained for the company. An executive of a company-sponsored grantmaking program commented: "My style is to try to staff the vice-president of the company, and if there is an opportunity, to make sure that he is the one who gets the limelight. I have some counterparts in other corporations that personally represent their corporation."

Visibility has both advantages and disadvantages. If publicity draws attention to controversial projects, it may be harder to maintain a favorable public image. The implication is that grantmaking decisions may be influenced by the perception of public reaction. This concern over image may explain why some foundations tend to fund only the most traditional projects. However, certain types of promotion can also help a constituency to understand the rationale for innovative grantmaking. A community foundation president said: "We're willing to take a chance. We say this to our donors too. We're in the risk business. We're going to do some things that look maybe a little more risky than you would do individually, but it is because the community needs it. That's our philosophy." Whatever the motives for encouraging publicity about foundation programs, most of the CEOs we interviewed considered networking and public relations a major part of their jobs.

Hours of Work

Foundation chief executives report long work hours. The majority (17) indicated that they work over 50 hours a week. Only two of the CEOs we interviewed say they spend less than 40 hours a week in the office. Most foundation executives indicate that they have little time to call their own. Foundation work is variable and characterized by periods of deadlines and pressures to prepare for board meetings. As one foundation president explained, the number of working hours depends on "the season, and whether there is a board deadline or not."

The very lifestyle of some foundation administrators revolves around their work. Many had difficulty estimating the amount of time they spend on the job because almost all their activities are work-related. A female president explained: "Well, frequently I'm up at six. I never count the time in hours, frankly, but I'll get home at ten [P.M.] five days a week, and I work a piece of a Saturday or Sunday, or both. But much of my life is interwoven, you see, with [work] interests." All the people she sees socially are also professional colleagues. In the evening she often dines with them, and the conversation usually centers on work. A male president with a similar schedule said:

> I haven't stopped to think lately, but I would be a little hard pressed to defend myself against charges of being a workaholic. But I do work, and have as long as I can remember, very long hours. So that I suppose my average day would be eleven or twelve hours. And that includes weekends with rare exceptions. Taking a whole weekend off is really rare.

Most of these chief executives report exhausting hours, but few indicated that they felt overworked.

Although some of the program officers reported that they work over 40 hours a week, they spend less time on the job than their bosses. Program officers usually attend fewer work-related social functions and entertain less. However, seven of the program officers we interviewed said that they work over 50 hours a week. One such individual complained: "You're getting at sore points. I think I've been putting in sixty-five or seventy hours a week. I'm in a mood for reducing my schedule. I typically work evenings and weekends."

All of the administrative assistants we interviewed work regular hours, usually less than 40 but more than 37 hours a week. They have specific tasks to perform, which they generally manage to complete in the office. None of them are involved with entertaining, social engagements, or interaction with others in the field. They occasionally work overtime during a crunch, or just before a board meeting, but report this as a rare occurrence.

Summary

Foundation staff give money away within the prestigious framework of institutions of philanthropy. Applicants assume some form of supplicant posture; reviewers receive requests, whether grandly or humbly, as their prerogative. Foundation executives enjoy high status because of their nominal control over allocations. Through their brokering and networking activities, CEOs and some program officers have the visibility and opportunity to influence others, an activity usually associated with wealthy philanthropists. Executives are generally served by support staff willing to do so without the serious recognition required for career advancement. However, most participants have the sense of doing exciting, worthwhile work on the cutting edge of social change.

Foundation staff have relatively little accountability for their decisions. In consequence, it cannot be known if they have sifted through the pool of applicants impartially, or whether they have specially promoted favored grantees. Further, the projects that have received support are rarely evaluated in a systematic or public fashion.

This description of the daily routine at foundations for the hierarchy of employees does not sufficiently highlight the privileged nature of the work. The structure of job duties confers status, especially on executives. Further discussion in later chapters will present additional dimensions of this privilege.

4

Recruitment and Career Paths

The foundation field may be a congenial pocket of opportunity for some fortunate employees, but access to this occupational area is quite limited. Although more positions have opened up in recent years, the grantmaking community is still relatively small and interconnected. Almost all the foundation employees we interviewed obtained their positions because they were familiar with the field, had a contact at a foundation, or knew someone who did. Age, gender, and type of education contribute to the formation of personal and professional networks, and older men with elite school ties and national reputations tend to be selected for prestigious foundation jobs.

Several grantmakers specifically mentioned the importance of networks in alerting them to openings for positions they now hold. The president of a foundation commented: "I think one of the secrets of getting a job is to let everybody know what kind of job you want." Another CEO said: "I had a friend who had his ear very close to the ground. He called me up." The chief executive of a company-sponsored foundation said: "I used my contacts in the company to get this job. I had a lot of contacts."

Foundation staff members have worked in academia, business, the nonprofit community, and the professions; some established their careers in philanthropy. The grantmakers we interviewed had been in the labor force an average of 23 years and had usually made at least one major career change. Many had volunteer experience as well. Most had formed some prior affiliation with the foundation through fundraising, consulting, or serving on a committee that reviews proposals.

For those who became CEOs, entry may have come fairly late in a distinguished career, when they were recruited for the job. Executives of foundations have normally held a wide variety of positions prior to their foundation appointments. In the 1982 *CB Survey*, 19 percent of the men and 3 percent of the women held positions equivalent to a CEO immediately before assuming their current roles. Almost one third of these men now receive salaries of over $100,000, illustrating the high status of the persons who are chosen to be executives of the largest foundations.

Selection Versus Open Application in the Foundation Field

According to study participants, high-level grantmaking positions are rarely advertised, but are acquired, as one CEO indicated, "through a version of the 'old boy network.'" The most prestigious candidates are "tapped"; they do not need to apply. They may not even deign to apply. The president of a large independent foundation said: "As far as I know the job was never advertised in any way. If it had been, it wouldn't have occurred to me to apply." Over half of the staff members we interviewed were recruited for their foundation positions without initiating a job search. An executive director remembered the circumstances surrounding his recruitment:

> I knew the foundation because I knew the former executive director. He was a friend of mine. And I knew the foundation anyway for the excellent work it had done. The individual who called me was a headhunter. But I know where my name came from. I've known a member of the board for a long time. He is also a member of the board of the [organization where I had worked]. I guess he suggested my name as a possible candidate. I met with the selection committee which was composed of five members of the board. I met with them twice, and it wasn't more than six weeks and they offered me the job.

Foundation employees who actively sought grantmaking work were also assisted by personal contacts. Access to networks for learning about and obtaining positions in the foundation world is of utmost importance.

Age has a bearing on recruitment for foundation positions, particularly when administrative assistants are deleted from the sample (see Table 5). The older the employee, the greater is the likelihood of recruitment for the job. Younger foundation staff members tend to have applied directly for their positions. There is an interrelationship between age and gender, as most female foundation employees are younger than their male counterparts. Older men with more work experience have had more opportunities to develop networks.

Gender is a major explanatory variable which accounts for differences between those asked to consider a grantmaking job and those applying directly. Almost 87 percent (all but three) of the men in the sample were invited to apply

for their current jobs by a member of the board. In contrast, thirty-nine percent (10) of the women were recruited for their positions (see Table 6). All but
one of the men (22) in the sample were either referred to the foundation or
learned of an opening through a network, whereas 43 percent of the women
(11) used other application methods. Women actively pursued foundation employment, and then attempted to advance within the field, while men were often brought into the top positions at large foundations after service in another
career area.

In addition, there is a hidden advantage for job applicants who attended elite
educational institutions. Recommendations of professors and alumni affiliations
were often reported as helpful in obtaining foundation positions. A program officer commented:

Table 5. Direct Application by Age (Interview Sample)

Application Source	Under 30	31–40	41–50	51–60	61–70	Total
Advertisement/Agency	1	2	1	0	0	4
	33%	15%	8%	0	0	8%
Letter/Personal Visit	1	3	3	1	0	8
	33%	23%	23%	6%	0	16%
Network Contacts	0	5	0	2	0	7
	0	39%	0	13%	0	14%
Recruited	1	3	9	13	4	30
	33%	23%	69%	81%	100%	61%
Total	3	13	13	16	4	49
	6%	27%	27%	33%	8%	100%

NOTE: Administrative Assistants Excluded.

Table 6. Direct Application by Gender (Interview Sample)

Application Source	Women	Men	Total
Advertisement/Agency	4	0	4
	16%	0	8%
Letter/Personal Visit	7	1	8
	27%	4%	16%
Network Contacts	5	2	7
	19%	9%	14%
Recruited	10	20	30
	39%	87%	61%
Total	26	23	49
	53%	47%	100%

NOTE: Administrative Assistants Excluded

There were some very loose, collegial, and other ties between the foundation and people I knew. For instance, a professor that I had in graduate school was a regular consultant to the foundation. I'm not sure what role he played in my getting the job. I think I might have had him down as a reference. One of the reasons that the job was posted at the university in the first place was that a member of our board was chairman of the university board. I think that the fact that I was an alumnus probably didn't hurt.

Another program officer discussed the referral methods used in his case: "The person that recruited for the original position I had with the foundation was looking for a young lawyer. He called the major law professors at Harvard, Yale, Columbia, and asked for recommendations of people who fit the description he gave."

The executive director of a family foundation explained how he obtained his position:

In a typically capricious way. A board member of this foundation kept asking me to do it. This is quite common in foundations dominated by family. They're looking for people likely to be comfortable with them. And it is not likely to be someone that they [board members] didn't know before. Professional talent is too far removed from that personal tie. Nobody came out of a competitive job search in this area. There is no one who did not have some personal connection, no matter how tenuous. They never run advertisements for jobs. The way I was hired is common.

When asked how she had obtained her present position, a woman executive replied:

Previously they had done it very privately. They did ask a number of people for recommendations of names, and apparently my name came up from many sources, not just one or two. And, it was a surprise, as the chair told me, that a woman's name would appear so many times. So they asked to talk to me, and from that evolved some conversations. It happened in a very informal way. But it was a heavy competition.

In contrast to men, women executives are generally recruited from within the field of foundation philanthropy.

Potential foundation staff members may be identified during the search process or had been on earlier occasions when the foundation was in need of specific expertise. Several study participants indicated that they had worked for the foundation as consultants before becoming permanent employees. A program officer described her own recruitment process. She said:

When I was a consultant they decided to replace the person who had left. There were two people here at the time who felt that they should do a search. They knew me, and they didn't want to be biased. I was one of the five finalists, and there were three interviews, because they had trouble deciding. I had thought about what I would do to develop a program, and the changes I would make. In this respect, I had an advantage over the other candidates.

This employee provides a good example of how an inside track is established. She is not suggesting that the recruitment process was rigged to favor a preferred candidate. But she does illustrate how prior connections and access before a position actually arises can be very advantageous.

Most of the respondents were familiar with grantmaking organizations. CEOs were the most knowledgeable, since they have the longest work careers and the best networks of those in the sample. One president commented: "Oh yes. I've known a lot of people at the Rockefeller Foundation, the Ford Foundation. . . . Almost every one of the foundations concerned with my field, the presidents of these, are friends of mine of long standing." When asked if he had been looking for a foundation position, this same president replied:

Well, I won't say that I had never thought about it. I know that in talking with my wife about what to do when I decided I had had enough of higher education administration, I told her that there was only one job that might be interesting to me, and that would be to be the head of a foundation. I thought it would be very appealing because you'd have a chance to really do something different.

Three CEOs had received foundation grants. A woman executive director explained:

I had been calling on foundations for years. I knew all the executives and officers. They were old friends. I had reached the point where they would regard my proposals favorably, because they knew I would have done the research, and made the right preparation. And, of course, people give money to people they know very often.

Program officers and administrative assistants were less familiar than CEOs with philanthropy before they accepted their current positions. Only two program officers indicated that they were quite knowledgeable about foundations, and both had received grants. A program officer who began her foundation career as a secretary said:

> I went for an interview at an employment agency. They said, "This is the
> ——— Foundation." And I didn't have the foggiest idea. I went home and
> asked a friend, "What is it?" She said, "You know, the Ford Foundation.
> Well, I imagine it is similar to that." That is how ignorant I was.

Most of the administrative assistants in the sample were uninformed about grantmaking until they received their first foundation positions.

Another entry to grantmaking comes through volunteer work. Most foundation staff members were well-connected within the nonprofit community prior to becoming foundation employees. Two thirds of the executives had been board members of nonprofit organizations. Over 40 percent of the total sample served as officers on community, regional, national, and professional organizations.

Those we interviewed tended to have volunteered their time to the more traditional nonprofit enterprises such as churches, hospitals, and political campaigns. They often mentioned the United Way and the YMCA. A chief executive officer described his previous volunteer work:

> My past activities were eight years as chairman of a committee for the
> United Way and six years as an officer. I was also on the board of ———
> Hospital for ten years, and was the chairman of the long-range planning
> committee, and on the finance committee. I was chairman of the YMCA for
> fifteen years, and I was on the Council Board of the Boy Scouts of America
> for twelve years.

Several women explained that they had gained much of their "professional" experience through volunteer work. A program officer discussed her previous unpaid work. She said:

> There was a period before I went back to school when I was very heavily in-
> volved in the League of Women Voters, for example, and some other com-
> mittees also, and where I spent half of my time. I probably could have had a
> paid job. But I could do it when it was very convenient, and I could fit it in.
> I think the volunteer work was very helpful in giving me confidence in deal-
> ing with people, strengthening my abilities.

Volunteer activities augment an individual's professional experiences and are often considered essential for foundation work. In addition, such activities bring individuals into networks that include foundation officials. However, men tend to be board members in larger and more prestigious nonprofit organizations and thus develop a broader range of contacts, while women are involved in smaller, community-based programs (McPherson and Smith-Lovin 1982).

We interviewed only 23 staff members (40 percent) who had acquired their jobs after applying for them directly. Only six of the CEOs (22 percent) initiated the application for their positions; and in one case the candidate had also been referred for the job. In comparison, twelve program officers (56 percent) and seven administrative assistants (70 percent) obtained their jobs after answering an advertisement, applying at an employment agency, writing an unsolicited letter, personally visiting the foundation, or hearing about the opening from a network contact during their job search.

Unlike other foundation employees, administrative assistants are often hired through advertisements and employment agencies. But they also use networks to find jobs. One of them explained:

> I had been in my job for eight years. I was thoroughly familiar with it and I felt that I needed a change. I went to many job interviews, until one day the woman that I worked directly under suggested that I contact ——— to see if she knew anything. She happened to know that the vice-president's own secretary was retiring, and that the vice-president was looking for someone.

Program officers usually are not recruited for their jobs, but they often hear about them through informal networks or use such ties when applying for foundation positions. Eight of the program officers we interviewed had also visited foundations, written letters expressing interest in employment, and responded to advertisements. One explained the importance of initiative in this process: "I learned about the foundation and got my résumé in there, basically. They weren't advertising any job openings, but I interviewed and I was offered a job. They didn't seek me out." Another program officer had been working as the director of a community agency and gradually realized that a publicized opening might suit her:

> I think three different young people came and asked me to write them a recommendation for this job. And I did, and none of them received the job. And then I just happened to look at a copy of the job description, which I hadn't done before. And it just dawned on me that it would be an awfully nice thing to be doing. So I applied, and I was one of three finalists, and was offered the job.

Most of the women in the sample directly applied for their jobs. Even when administrative assistants are omitted, sixteen women (62 percent) said that they had initiated a job search which eventually led to a foundation position. They told acquaintances in personal and professional networks that they were looking for work, wrote letters and enclosed résumés to grantmaking organizations, answered advertisements, and applied at employment agencies. These accounts reinforce what we already know: women are not as well tied in to influential networks as are men; and so women work harder, using any access to desired positions.

Education

Although work experience is often an acceptable substitute, a college education, or even an advanced degree, seems required for every kind of foundation
job. Almost all of the foundation chief executives and program officers in the
sample are college educated, and over 65 percent have earned advanced degrees (see Table 7).

Table 7. Position by Level of Education (Interview Sample)

Position	Less Than B.A.	B.A.	Some Graduate Work	M.A.	J.D., M.D., Ph.D.	Total
Chief Executive Officer	1	7	3	8	7	26
	14%	44%	75%	47%	47%	44%
Program Officer	1	5	0	9	8	23
	14%	31%	0%	53%	53%	39%
Administrative Assistant	5	4	1	0	0	10
	71%	25%	25%	0	0	17%
Total	7	16	4	17	15	59
	12%	27%	7%	29%	25%	100%

Table 8. Gender by Education (Interview Sample)

	Less Than B.A.	B.A.	Some Graduate Work	M.A.	J.D., M.D., Ph.D.	Total
Women	1	9	2	10	3	25
	50%	75%	67%	59%	20%	51%
Men	1	3	1	7	12	24
	50%	25%	33%	41%	80%	49%
Total	2	12	3	17	15	49
	4%	24%	6%	36%	30%	100%

NOTE: Administrative assistants excluded.

Men in the interview sample are somewhat more highly educated than the
women. Only two women in any position have Ph.D.s, in comparison with
eight men, a finding corroborated by the results of the 1982 *CB Survey* (Boris
and Hooper 1982). About half of the professional women have degrees beyond
the B.A. (see Table 8). Three of the women we interviewed said they had been
enrolled in doctoral programs, but as one CEO explained: "I went up to the
thesis and never completed it." Only one male program officer did not complete a doctoral program, once begun.

The possession of an advanced degree is significantly correlated with higher
salaries among CEOs in the 1982 *CB Survey* data. Of the 22 CEOs with the
highest salaries, fifteen (68 percent) have J.D., M.D., or Ph.D. degrees, and

over three quarters work for the largest foundations. While almost half of women CEOs have gone beyond the B.A., only four (9 percent) of the female CEOs in the *CB Survey* sample have degrees beyond the master's level while 51 (38 percent) of the men do. After asset or equivalent grant level, degree status is the variable most strongly correlated with CEO salary level (see Appendix 1).

Foundation employees tend to graduate from private colleges and universities. Over half (55 percent) of the staff members in the interview sample who have degrees received them from such educational institutions; approximately 20 percent of these individuals graduated from Ivy League universities (see Table 9).

The hiring practices of foundations in different regions vary. The status of the educational institution from which an employee graduated seems to have more influence in the East, especially in the more established foundations. However, the status attributed to institutions also varies by region, and large state universities have more prestige in the Midwest and West. In New York City, where the largest number of foundations are concentrated, seventy-five percent of staff members were educated at private schools; two thirds of all the individuals we interviewed who had graduated from Ivy League universities work in New York City. But foundation personnel in California are more likely to have received their degrees from state colleges and universities.

Grantmaking programs often have some bearing on selection of foundation employees educated within particular disciplines. For example, if a foundation funds in the arts, employees who are hired usually have some education or experience in arts and the humanities. But generally, the discipline of origin is not as important as the legitimation produced by some form of higher education. Staff members at foundations hold degrees in fields as diverse as English and microbiology. An executive director explained: "I don't think it makes any difference what your educational background is. It could be social work, or sociology, or psychology. It could be anything in the arena of business administration. A lot of foundation executives are attorneys. There's a whole wide range."

Table 9. Position by Status of Educational Institution Where Highest Degree Was Received (Interview Sample)

Position	Ivy League	Other Private	State-Supported	Total
Chief Executive Officer	3	18	5	26
	50%	49%	50%	49%
Program Officer	3	14	5	22
	50%	38%	50%	42%
Administrative Assistant	0	5	0	5
	0	13%	0	9%
Total	6	37	10	53
	11%	70%	19%	100%

Many foundation personnel are working in funding areas that are quite different from those they studied in college.

In the interview sample, the highest percentage (39 percent) of participants were educated in the social sciences, followed by the arts and humanities (25 percent) (see Table 10). The women we interviewed are more likely to have degrees in the social sciences and humanities than men. More men have business and legal training.

The *CB Survey* data also suggest that advanced degrees are important for the prestigious, highly compensated CEO positions, but the subject field studied is not correlated with salary level. However, the proportion of foundation executives with social science backgrounds who also have salaries of more than $80,000 is greater than for other areas of study.

Career Paths

Chief executive officers are older, thus tend to have had more employment experience than other foundation staff members. But as an indication of the diversity found in the field, most foundation employees have had four or five prior jobs and changed their occupational areas at least once before entering philanthropy. The staff members we interviewed had worked at the same grantmaking organization for from less than one to over 30 years. The average time spent at a foundation is eight years; half of the participants have worked for their current employer five years or less. On average, they have had two jobs in the same organization. Eight CEOs in the interview sample had been promoted into their positions. Twelve program officers and three administrative assistants had been employed in other capacities at either the same or another foundation before accepting their current jobs.

Foundation men are more likely than women to have made a major career change during their working lifetimes. All of the men we interviewed said that they had decided to change career areas at least once. Every individual's career

Table 10. Position by Type of Educational Field (Interview Sample)

Position	Arts and Humanities	Business	Law	Social Sciences	Sciences	Other	Total
Chief Executive Officer	6	3	2	11	2	1	25
	43%	100%	50%	50%	50%	10%	44%
Program Officer	5	0	2	11	1	3	22
	36%	0	50%	50%	25%	30%	39%
Administrative Assistant	3	0	0	0	1	6	10
	21%	0	0	0	25%	60%	17%
Total	14	3	4	22	4	10	57
	25%	5%	7%	39%	7%	17%	100%

path is unique, but several foundation CEOs aspired to be, or were, both academics and journalists at one time in their lives. The following description by an executive director of his early career goals and employment background is illustrative of the variety in CEOs' experience before they became grantmakers.

> When I got out of college I had a sort of tweedy image, because I went to college with a lot of tweedy professors, and I admired them. I sort of thought then that maybe I would be realized some day as a pipe-smoking professor. Then that idea got changed. I worked in a number of other places, which all had their own perspectives. One very powerful one was newspaper work, which is kind of blue-collar life. You turn out a product every day. The people are kind of tough smart, rather than fragile smart. They are more the rough and tumble, and I like that.

Over half of the male foundation employees we interviewed had made two or more career changes. More than half of the women had made one career change; but only eight women (23.5 percent) had made two or more career changes. A fifth of the women in the sample have always worked in philanthropy, whereas none of the men had this pattern.

Most of the administrative assistants we interviewed have always worked in the clerical field. One of them commented:

> I've been working for twenty years, and I'm older than the school of hotshot ladies now. I am jaded enough to know the reality of things. I have always been treated very well, everywhere I worked, but I was still a secretary. I don't have any great ambition about my career. I'm really very satisfied to be here.

Clerical career patterns in philanthropy mirror those in the larger occupational world.

The recruitment of men and women from higher education into philanthropic work also reflects the status hierarchy in education itself. Men are in the higher-status supervisory positions. Most of the men in the interview sample with backgrounds in academia had been higher-education administrators. They were university officers, deans, chancellors, provosts, or presidents before becoming foundation CEOs or program officers. In contrast, the women had been assistant professors, graduate teaching assistants, and secretaries.

Although not all foundation executives were university presidents at one time, the proportion is high enough to support that stereotype. Some of the men who had been CEOs of both a university and a foundation commented that the jobs had many similarities. One explained:

I think that it is very understandable, and that it has been going on for a very long time. I think the jobs are really quite comparable: CEO over a university and CEO of a foundation are used to dealing with people from a range of disciplines, most of which are unfamiliar to them. A guy might come out of history, but he is dealing with physicists, and so you learn how to deal with intellectual projects, or types of ideas that are outside your own. You become a generalist. The range of contacts that an executive officer of an institution is likely to have is pretty broad. And then finally, the basic job of a foundation and a university is the same. I ought to add that they both know how to work with a board, and they both can work with staff that have areas of expertise. The administrative skills are very comparable, but I think the most important task of any university person is to allocate scarce resources, and that means finding people, identifying good ideas. I don't think there is anything unique about a foundation job, but of all the jobs I could think about, the job that comes closest at this general level is academic work.

The same foundation executive felt that his current job is "much, much simpler; much less complex; much less stress; fewer constituencies that you have to please. And, it's much harder to make a mistake." An important point to stress then, and an element of the congenial pocket of work in the foundation field, is the lack of "heat" (as in public criticisms and unfavorable press) and public accountability in these jobs. As one executive said:

> We don't have a constituency. We don't have stockholders. We don't have members. So that whatever sense of responsibility we feel and manifest is from within. It is not externally developed. So there are relatively few external forces which we have to contend with, although that has changed a bit in the last few years. This situation is without parallel in modern society, as far as I am concerned.

A majority (88 percent) of the sample have worked continuously since they accepted their first paid positions. However, seven women interrupted their careers for homemaking and motherhood. All of them were out of the labor force at least six years while raising their children. Most of these individuals are program officers. One of them explained:

> I was a housewife. I graduated from college, got married, and had kids; stayed home for several years, and with the exception of one part-time job, during a few of those years, didn't work in the paid world. I went back to get my master's degree when my youngest child was in the first grade.

Only one CEO had an interrupted career path. She had been a volunteer as her children were growing up, and eventually served on a number of boards of nonprofit organizations. She said: "I taught school like everybody else. For two or three years before I came here I was aware that I was bored. I had not worked for twenty years. I had stayed at home and reared three children."

These patterns of movement and stability in careers reflect the opportunity structure of employment open to men and women, as well as individual perceptions of opportunity. Men have more options than women and can advance their careers through a variety of alternatives, while they experiment with occupational interests and styles at the same time. Women are more cautious because options are more restricted. Better or even good jobs may be hard to find, and so women stay where they are.

However, the philanthropic world does offer some opportunity for career mobility not readily available elsewhere. At least three women CEOs in the sample started their careers as secretaries. One indicated: "Well, it was such a surprise to get this job. I'm a real fifties girl. I didn't expect really to have a career, and the greatest luck put me into this position." Twenty-seven study participants (45 percent) have worked in the grantmaking field ten years or longer or have held several different foundation positions. The president of a large foundation, who has been there over ten years, said:

> I have changed jobs every five years prior to this one, and this has been longer. One answer may be that at this stage in life stability is a good thing. Maybe it's that within this job there's enough variety so that you get some renewal. Or maybe none of the above. One really shouldn't stay much longer. And I really don't know the answer. When I took the job I thought that I would be gone by now. And I'm not gone. I like my work.

Another president who has been in philanthropy even longer reminisced:

> I'll tell you the absolute truth. I have worked in the foundation field since the 1950s. For the first twenty years I literally never thought of myself as a foundation officer. I thought that I was working with ideas, and I happened to be at a foundation. I had never seen it as a profession in that sense. And I still, to some degree, don't. I've changed my sense of direction on the issue. I think that it's very important to have people running foundations who have a basic understanding of human organization, and some knowledge of management. It is a big business today, regardless of how large the foundation is. And so I believe that there are some qualifications, but not necessarily foundation background that's important.

According to the 1982 *CB Survey*, a larger proportion of CEOs seem to be coming from within foundation philanthropy. Those with previous foundation backgrounds accounted for 30 percent of responding CEOs. In all, close to 40 percent of CEOs have come from the nonprofit sector, a new development (Boris and Hooper 1982). Women in the sample were more likely than men to have pursued philanthropic careers, and they have had more mobility within the field. Six out of the eight CEOs who had been promoted into their positions from another job at the same foundation were women. Most men are recruited for the CEO position. Only one man had worked his way up to the executive job and even he had entered at a fairly advanced level. Another man told us that his promotion was really a change in title, rather than an increase in responsibilities.

At least ten (seven women and three men) of the foundation staff members we interviewed had held several positions within the same foundation. For example, one woman had initially been hired as a program assistant, had progressed to program associate, and then to her present position as a program officer. She said:

> I would say that no competition was involved. We are very small here. We don't have a particular number of slots to be filled. So that it was a change of title to recognize that I had been doing program officer work for quite a long time. I had obviously developed more responsibility and more competence and had taken on more things. The first title change was totally initiated by my superiors. The more recent change was one that I had expressed some interest in.

Two additional program officers had been promoted from positions as secretaries at their foundations. Four other program officers had been consultants to their foundations prior to becoming permanent employees. Another individual began as a program officer and was promoted to assistant director.

According to the 1982 *CB Survey* data, women program officers on the whole have less seniority than men. While a high proportion of both genders have been in their foundations less than two years (32 percent of the men; 46 percent of the women), a larger proportion of men (45 percent) than women (24 percent) have been in their grantmaking organizations more than five years. A high proportion of both men and women have also been in their current positions for less than two years: 50 percent of male program officers and 62 percent of female program officers. However, on the average, women receive lower salaries regardless of their length of service (see Appendix 1).

While some people rise through one foundation, others switch foundations for career advancement. Seven grantmakers had changed foundations at one time in their career; six of them were women. Apparently, the picture of women seeking stability over opportunity can be misleading. When women see advancement opportunities in job transfers within the philanthropic arena, they may take them.

Most of the study participants who have been in the foundation field over ten years want to continue in foundation work. One president commented: "It kind of spoils you for anything else. Just because of the diversity, the freedom, the opportunity for creativity. It has so few limits. And almost any other job I can think of is much more narrow; there is likely to be much more of a bureaucracy; less freedom."

For *CB Survey* respondents, the number of years spent in the CEO position is not significantly correlated with salary level. The most highly paid foundation executives are recruited after a career in another occupational area, and therefore command top compensation upon entering the foundation. Among the 54 percent of CEOs who have been in their positions for five years or less are more than half of those earning salaries of at least $100,000 (see Appendix 1).

The number of years in a grantmaking organization and in a job are somewhat more important in explaining program officer salaries than in explaining CEO salaries. This implies that program officers spend more time in the organization, gaining experience in order to make higher salaries, while CEOs bring their experience with them.

Summary

There are no standardized career patterns in this area, but the preceding trends are indicative of different career styles. The foundation field is a relatively new occupational area and people enter it as generalists. They come not only from a variety of backgrounds, but with diverse career trajectories. Some patterns can be discerned in what we have reported in this chapter; others are implicit in the structure of opportunity described throughout this and the preceding chapters.

The way the work is organized makes a variety of career lines possible. One of the most interesting grows out of building opportunities: network contacts and structural circumstances, such as knowing someone on the staff or board, working as a support person until a better job opens up, or gaining the favor of someone highly placed who acts as a mentor or patron. Because the field is developing, status lines are often not yet rigidly formed and many foundations are still small and fluid organizations. These situations provide opportunities for women who are able to work hard and rise to higher positions when given the chance.

Volunteers form a second career path: social activists and committed Peace Corps or Vista workers, primarily men who enter the foundation field to continue careers doing relevant work in communities. Women form another volunteer cadre of careerists. They are community activists who may have been grantees of the foundation. They become known to the foundation board or staff because of work they are doing in areas that the foundation funds.

The third career path is that of distinguished academics who might be termed luminaries; these persons are recruited from prestigious positions to head the largest foundations. They are almost exclusively men. Sometimes this path resembles that of those close to or just beyond retirement who are looking for shorter, less strenuous assignments. Some foundation executive positions are seen as providing a restful sinecure for distinguished retirees after a lifetime of service in another area.

The newest career path is found primarily among women who choose philanthropy and actively seek to rise to positions of leadership. The number of jobs in the foundation field seems to be slowly increasing. There are more positions available in small and medium-sized foundations, and a few new large grantmaking organizations have formed. However, some opportunities may be closing down even as others have opened up. Most of the largest foundations are not growing, but cutting back on staff. Consequently, there may be fewer opportunities and stiffer competition for the most prestigious grantmaking jobs.

5

Problems Women Face
in Combining Personal Life
with Foundation Work

The women's movement has focused our awareness on the fact that women assume the major burden for integrating family life, as well as mediating between the family and the larger world. This focus has also led to an increased interest in the overall quality of life, as well as a heightened understanding of how much responsibility we expect women to bear for the production and maintenance of familial and social activities, and how these expectations may limit and obstruct women's opportunities in the labor market. These understandings have encouraged both social science researchers and policymakers to examine the relation between personal life and paid employment. Are we blaming the victim when we point to the difficulties many women have in reaching the higher levels of occupational hierarchies because of their commitments to home and family? What accommodations should employers provide for their workers with families? Should husbands and older children take more responsibility for homemaking? What assistance in child care facilities or tax breaks for working mothers should be sponsored by government? These questions have all received increasing attention in recent years.

In most contexts, the focus of concern has been on how well women can manage both work and family. Kanter (1977b) identified several aspects of paid employment that affect how well women are able to adjust to these demands. They include the degree to which an occupation absorbs workers' lives; the effects of time pressures, especially work hours and schedules; the rewards and resources provided by a job; the culture or worldview of an occupation; and the emotional climate at work (Kanter 1977b, pp. 25–51). All these considerations affect the family as well as the work setting. Family and personal responsibilities also influence an individual's performance on the job (Kanter 1977b, pp. 53–58). In this chapter, we consider the effect of job requirements and personal responsibilities on women and men in philanthropy.

Perhaps the clearest indication of differing gender-based perceptions of responsibility appears in views on personal and family matters. Responsibilities to spouse and family are easier for men than for women to manage while they pursue their careers. When we asked men if their personal or family situation had a bearing on their work or career options, they generally said no. And yet men in grantmaking are more likely than their women colleagues to be married and have children (see Tables 11 and 12). Most men in the sample are absorbed in work, and so they depend on their wives to provide comfortable homes and family life. In contrast, although they are also career oriented, most of the women in the sample spoke at great length about the problems of trying to balance work with personal responsibilities. Married women wondered if they spend enough time with their families. Younger single women expressed concern about whether or not they will marry and have children. Foundation women are keenly aware that they live in a transitional time period when gender roles are changing. But they are not sure how or whether these changes will permit them to enjoy fulfillment both at work and in their personal lives.

Striking differences in the marital status of the foundation men and women we interviewed suggest how little basic change this transitional period has yet created for men as compared with women. Men employed by grantmaking organizations almost always have wives, whereas foundation women are, regardless of age, just as likely to be single as married (see Table 11). Over half of the foundation women we interviewed are not currently married, while all but one of the male participants are married. All the foundation employees we interviewed who had never married (or who divorced and never remarried) are women. Six of the women who have always been single are "professionals" and five are administrative assistants. Commitment to a work career, clearly, must require some greater sacrifices of family commitment from women than it does from men.

Although societal pressures encourage both men and women to marry and have children, career women also face counter-pressures emanating from both professional and personal spheres. Many of the women we interviewed indicated that the most difficult career and personal situations involve how to combine work, marriage, and children. They claim that it is easier to be single and pursue a career or to be married without children or to rear children without a husband. They also face expectations that they will care for aged relatives or rear children in preference to marriage or remarriage.

Single foundation employees usually live alone, or with their children, or they reported responsibilities for older family members. The women who have never been married, or are currently divorced, separated, or widowed, span all age groups, suggesting that the problems of women attempting careers in the work force continue in the present to make work and family difficult to coordinate.

Young women see various aspects of this problem clearly, although they may not yet have decided how to resolve them. An unmarried program officer in her early thirties, who considers herself ambitious, is concerned about the effects of work on her personal life:

> I'm in New York principally for career reasons, but that affects my personal life because it means that I'm not in an environment that I like all that much. I have not figured out how to resolve that. . . . At the beginning of this job, for the first year or nine months, I did nothing but work. I lost all contact with my close friends. They would call me and I wouldn't return their telephone calls because I was working day and night.

That same program officer spoke of a man she is dating, whose work pattern is similar to hers. She touches on the problems of dual career couples who are almost totally work absorbed:

Table 11. Gender by Current Marital Status (Interview Sample)

Gender	Never Married	Married	Unmarried, but Living with Mate	Divorced, Separated, or Widowed	Total
Women	11	17	2	6	36
	100%	43%	100%	86%	60%
Men	0	23	0	1	24
	0	58%	0	14%	40%
Total	11	40	2	7	60
	18%	67%	3%	12%	100%

Table 12. Number of Children by Gender (Interview Sample)

Number of Children	Women	Percent	Men	Percent	Total	Percent
none	22	85%	4	15%	26	43%
one	3	60%	2	40%	5	8%
two	8	57%	6	43%	14	23%
three	1	14%	6	86%	7	12%
four	1	25%	3	75%	4	7%
five or more	1	25%	3	75%	4	7%
Total	36	60%	24	40%	60	100%

> I go out with a guy who is a [professional]. He doesn't have anything but
> me, a couple of hours on the weekend, and his work. . . . He doesn't have
> time for anything else. That's not a life. You can end your life. That's not
> what life is about. . . . So I'm trying to figure this stuff out.

Among the unresolved issues that women consider, then, is how anyone, not
just women, can regulate the press of work in a demanding job so that a well-
rounded life becomes possible.

One alternative that women can choose is consciously to renounce some of
the roles and responsibilities of family life, postponing or abandoning the possibility of having children, for example. Some women seem happy with this alternative. A female foundation president without children commented:

> We have no kids. I've been married for over thirty years to my husband.
> Our careers have complemented each other very much. He did a lot of trav-
> eling. Neither one of us is ever bored. We understand each other and do a
> lot of conversing. Before it was fashionable, he encouraged me. I was the
> first woman in the company to travel, to stay out of town overnight. He's
> never held me back, and became an excellent cook. We're supportive of
> each other.

Clearly, this alternative depends upon men who might still be considered un-
usual. A realistic outlook on marriage and family life might have to take into account husbands with more conventional expectations. A younger woman program officer, who is married but has no children, talked about how this
alternative worked for her: "I would say, first of all, the work impact on personal life is favorable. Having a job that you like as much as I like this one has
got to be important. The one aspect of my job that perhaps is less benign is
travel."

Although more options have become available in recent years, women still
feel conflict about adequately performing their family roles. The same program
officer hesitated and continued: "My husband really does not object to my traveling most of the time. He understands and he is supportive, and he takes care
of himself. But there are times when you wish that you didn't have to go away."
But then she said they are considering having children, and if they did the impact of her work on family life would change.

One program officer responded to the question about work and personal life
by commenting that she might never have children: "Well, I'm single right
now—some of which has been painful. I was married and divorced. I made a
decision not to have children because the relationship I was in wasn't right.
And I might not have children because I'll be too old. That is important, a big
consideration." Many of the younger women referred to the tensions between
career goals and the issue of having children, or even having that opportunity.

A single program officer was planning to marry in the near future. Her fiancé lives and works in another city. Although the distance has not been an overwhelming obstacle in maintaining their relationship, one of them will have to move if they are to live together. She said they had not yet resolved that question, although she tends to spend weekends at his house.

These dilemmas and decisions reflect the view that such problems are personal rather than social. Women see these issues as matters of responsibility and decision confronting them as women, rather than problems facing men or society in general. Realistically, then, women see the problem of a gender-stratified society as one in which they are at a disadvantage and must make all the adjustments in the expected direction—that is, male priorities in career and family arrangements come first, in the accepted order of things. Whatever changes are occurring in society to permit women greater opportunities in the workplace, readjustment of attitudes about the organization and direction of family life must also occur. But the women we interviewed indicated, directly or indirectly, that the tendency to give the man's career priority in our society is one they will ultimately have to accept.

Another foundation employee explained how she accepts that priority and how it affects her career options:

> The reason we moved was because of my husband's job, not mine. And I expect that if he lost his job tomorrow, well, I'm still working for the foundation, but chances are we would move because of his career, not because of mine. The other thing is that we are expecting [a] child. And that definitely has an effect on my job. I expect to probably come back part-time.

Yet another woman staff member commented: "I do not have any children yet—the big yet. So that I have not had to deal with all that juggling of child care and working hours so far." She said that she and her husband both recognize that she would have primary responsibility for child-rearing.

A female CEO who has worked in the field of philanthropy for over 30 years talked about the effects of child-rearing on her career. Although she employs a maid two days a week to do the laundry and house cleaning, she does all the cooking and shopping in the family. She commented philosophically: "If I had not had a family I would probably put my energy into something else." But she also said: "The hardest thing for me, having children, was the cutting off of my mobility."

One woman executive director had a child after she assumed her position. She said her whole work pattern changed. She discussed the hectic nature of her personal life, especially when she had to travel, and the "juggling that goes on in terms of child care responsibilities." And: "I was putting in a lot more hours before that, and I would continue to take work home, but I just said, 'I won't do it on weekends.'" She indicated:

I took off three and a half months, and then went back [to work] two days a week for a while, and then gradually went back to five days a week, which was fine with the board. It worked out really well. I advertised in the paper [for child care]. By the third person I found one that is just excellent. Everything [in the home] is done by other people. Quite literally. She does all my laundry. I have people clean. We have lawn services.

She and her husband are thinking about having another child, but she has reservations about balancing work and family. She continued:

I've witnessed with so many of my other friends, the women, that dual role that they have is very schizophrenic and so tension-producing. The need to be always competent, and on top of it, and working as hard as possible, and sometimes that translates into hours. There's a certain competitiveness within every office. I think any of these [foundation] jobs could expand to fill eighty hours a week if you wanted them to. A lot of the men have more opportunity to let it expand, because they have fewer responsibilities at home. And the women, I think there were a lot of pressures, and we just bear a lot more stress and tension. I think of my saying, "Oh God, it's six-thirty, I can't stay any longer. I've got to go home." That sort of thing. And then putting on an entirely different hat at home.

Another woman CEO, with an even younger child, said:

My husband is proud and supportive. And the fact that I have a baby means that I have less time to work. But that may be healthy, and in fact, I'm sure it is. My husband is supportive, but very definitely thinks that my work is less important than his. So we've had disagreements about who is responsible in the morning, and in the evening, and when she's sick. That is the biggest strain that I have had. I must say I went into this with my eyes open. I was willing to function as [if I were] a single parent, to do all the work. I didn't expect fifty percent help, and yet I wanted the baby anyway.

A program officer with older children discussed the guilt she felt at not being a full-time mother, but said that her children had supported her in her career:

When the boys were in high school they were both on the swim team. And there was a swim team mothers' group that took on the responsibilities of preparing spreads for our team and the visiting team after home meets. And the first time I was called to work on one of these I said, "Oh, I am really sorry, but I have to be in Washington on that day. It is part of my job. And I have to be there. I really would love to help. Please call me again." And they never did. And it really bothered me. I felt I was back in high school, and wasn't asked to join the top sorority. So one morning I was driving the boys over to swim team practice about seven-thirty in the morning. I was going to work. And I told the boys about this. "I really do want to help, and

I feel terrible that they haven't called me." And one of my sons said, "Mother, you're kidding. You really feel terrible?" And I said, "Yeah, I do. I feel kind of awful about that." And he leaned over and said, "Mom, don't feel terrible. Don't you realize that those women, that's all they have to do. And look at you, and all you have."

All my working life I have had that—you know, in the back of your head there is a little guilt there because maybe you are not doing as well by your children as you should be. And all that stuff that people are trying to lay on you. And it all just washed off. I mean, I lost it right there. Because I thought, "My kid understands. His is proud of me." I never had to worry about that ever again. I can remember the entire moment.

Other foundation women said that they had stayed at home with their children until they were older. One program officer commented:

I stayed home, because my generation did that, until my youngest child was in junior high school. When I look back on it, it sounds amazing to me, you know, that was fifteen years, and I had a master's degree and all. I did volunteer work. But I think having a supportive family is real helpful.

And another said: "I deliberately chose to stay home because I believe that it was better for the kids, better for me, if I were with them."

But whether women made the decision to sacrifice or postpone career opportunities for children and family, or made the reverse sacrifice, it is clear that they see the decision as a personal one. At best, it is one worked out with some accommodation from family. In consequence, the world of employment, including the foundation world, has never been asked to make much accommodation for women or men employees with families.

Both men and women workers in the middle class who do have families respond to the pressure of the work world and the desire for higher living standards by restricting family size. Foundation employees are no exception to this general pattern. Even though foundation employees have diverse family arrangements, family size tends to be small. But the men in the sample are more likely than the women to have children, and larger families as well. Over 83 percent of the men we interviewed in grantmaking are fathers, and only 39 percent of the foundation women are mothers (see Table 12).

In the interview sample, more than half (55 percent) of the women CEOs do not have children, but only two (12.5 percent) of the male chief executives are childless. Half of the women program officers are not mothers, whereas only two (25 percent) of the male program officers are not fathers. Most of the administrative assistants (80 percent) are childless. The younger women in the sample may still make the decision to have children, but it is also possible that their current decisions will remain firm.

Although male grantmakers are husbands and family men, they tend to conform to the traditional pattern of entrusting child care and home life to their wives, even if they also work. Most of the men in the sample are older than the women, and this pattern may help account for the more conventional family arrangements men exhibit. However, even younger foundation men claim they are less involved than their wives with their children. The comments of two chief executive officers in their forties are illustrative. A foundation president said:

> My work obviously gives me status in the community, which to an extent is a positive thing. I work pretty hard to try and have some time for my kids. I think my wife made a decision some time ago to quit work at least until the children reached a certain point. And I think that that's been a strain on her. And I think that, you know, it's not atypical. It's a fairly classic problem nowadays. I didn't encourage her not to work. In fact, I encouraged her to work if that was what she wanted. But she feels that at least until the children reach a certain age that she needs to be at home as a full-time parent. It's often unspoken but I know she feels that she's given up a lot from a career point of view. And even though she's doing what she feels she wants to, there's still a sense of loss and resentment, and those sorts of things. And I think to an extent, at least the fact that my job is so encompassing, and so overpowering, is a little intimidating.

This man indirectly acknowledges his acceptance of an inequitable system in which he is the beneficiary—and one which he has no need to question. The amount of real encouragement a man in his position can actually give his wife to work if she wished, for instance, is debatable. Without a support structure to help her maintain the home and provide child care, she really has no option. But her husband's recognition of her resentment is not one which causes him to reconsider his own strategy for integrating work and family. He "tries" to have time for the kids. But implicit in his remarks is the expectation that he can rely on his wife if he cannot do it. Another male CEO gives the same impression that he would like to be more accommodating if it were possible. But he says quite clearly that he doesn't worry much about it. "I've never felt that my family helped or hindered my professional development. Oh, sometimes I felt that I haven't given them the support and development that I could because I was off chasing my job. But I don't stay on that too long. You know, I'm not overly wrought."

One way to rationalize the problem of inequitable family arrangements, at least in the forum of the interview, is to stress the value of the support provided by a wife. The foundation executives in their fifties and sixties all mentioned how much they have depended on and admired their wives. One commented:

> Mine is a very intelligent wife, with whom I like to discuss things. So, I may tell her what I am thinking about, or give her the first draft of the president's report to see if it makes sense to her. She is a good critic. And there are a lot of things that we [the foundation] are interested in that are interesting to her. All my life I've been able to talk about my work with my wife.

Another explained: "I think that my ability to perform at whatever level I am performing is due principally to my wife."

In the same way that wives are valued, children may be discussed as of great importance, even though they do not receive priority attention. A foundation president with grown children expressed the sentiments of many of his peers about children:

> I am very fascinated by—in love with—concerned about my children. I value those relationships enormously. Obviously we don't see each other a whole lot, or in a very leisurely fashion when we do. But let me just say that I value them enormously, and it's a part of my emotional life that's very important.

Not all family patterns reported by male informants resemble the most traditional expectations of the division of labor between husband and wife. Several male foundation employees mentioned that their wives work, but only two spoke about the issues surrounding a dual career family. A CEO whose wife is an academic said: "Our notion was that we each wanted to be in a position where we could be fired over principle or quit." And a program officer commented: "We are a two-career family. We are both at about the same plane in our careers. If one of us would get an offer to go to Washington, it would be a real strain."

Most of the men we interviewed thought that their families approved of their work. But few questioned the primacy of work as a value in life. One foundation employee believes that his job had a negative bearing on his family life. He said: "My former wife felt that there were periods, particularly many years when we had very young children, when I was traveling a lot and she was suffering burdens by virtue of my traveling." And another foundation executive said: "[Marriage] has given me a real balance in terms of the importance of my time. My work used to be too important."

Only one male foundation employee, a program officer, said that he participates equally with his wife in child-rearing. And he is also the only man who clearly said that his career decisions would be influenced by his family responsibilities. He explained:

> I place a very high value on the family, so I would decline career options to travel extensively or stay away from the family for long intervals, or a job that reduced access to the family. I wouldn't take such a job at this point in

the development of the family. But there is some amount of tension gener-
ated anyway. I feel so strongly about coparenting, even though the process
is tiring and frustrating. [It is] such an important part of my identity that I
do my best to shuffle back and forth, and that can be depleting. But it is satisfying to the other side of the person.

These comments were similar to many made by women with children in the
study: major commitments to both career and family are almost impossible to
maintain.

Options available to married men and women in foundation work are clearly
very different, with different costs and benefits attached to job commitment.
The options for single women offer another set of alternatives. Two widely varying views on commitment to the job are represented by the following.

One of the unmarried administrative assistants in the sample indicated that
her life is centered around her work and her boss. "I find that my entire life is
around him [the president of the foundation]. It's definitely the center. I sometimes come out of here at night, and it's rough."

But not all the single foundation employees we interviewed lead job-cen-
tered lives. Although she is the exception, another administrative assistant said
she consciously selected a less demanding occupation, and has even turned
down other opportunities, so that she can pursue her avocation. Her situation is
similar to other actors, artists, musicians, and writers.

> My primary interest in life is my creative work. I have chosen not to be-
> come a professional in that field, to be independent of the marketplace.
> Therefore, I have to have work to support this hobby, or whatever you want
> to call it. So I have always sought employment that would make my primary
> interest more attainable, not put obstacles in my way as far as working a
> great deal of overtime, or expending a great deal of nervous energy on the
> job. That kind of energy I would rather reserve for my own private work.

She said that she is single because she prefers the flexibility of not having family
responsibilities. Single women, like single men, now have opportunities to create lifestyles around work or work around lifestyles.

But women who become single after marriage face a different set of issues.
The anxieties and pressures of a divorce, separation, or the death of a spouse almost always have repercussions in working life. Such tragedies affect both men
and women, but when there are children in the family, the impact on women
may be greater because they usually are granted custody and continue primary
responsibility for child-rearing. The two men we interviewed who had been divorced said they are now happily remarried. The children from their first mar-
riages continue to live with the former wives. Although both noted that they
had been divorced, neither man elaborated on any personal or employment-
related problems they might have encountered at the time. However, one of

the women program officers who was already working when she and her husband separated commented: "The sense of grief and loss was sort of paralyzing. And my work was really slower in coming, and less focused. It seemed to be beyond my control."

Divorce can be even more devastating to those women who then become displaced homemakers. Another female program officer in the sample had sought employment during her divorce proceedings. She said: "I was desperately in need of a job, and I had two children to support. I needed to find something quickly that was fairly lucrative, so I would have enough funds to maintain the household." Prior to the divorce she had been a full-time homemaker. She remembered: "I had no intention of going to work. I was going to stay home and be mother and hostess." She has now made a successful career, and her children are older. But she indicated: "When my children were younger, it was terribly important, there was a need for security to know that I was going to be able to take care of them."

A woman chief executive officer commented: "I'm divorced. And a job becomes the central focus of one's life. I still have a child who lives with me." Balancing home life with work is difficult, particularly for employed women with children.

Summary

Once again, the problems foundation women face in trying to combine satisfying careers with personal life reflect patterns in larger society. However, because of their flexibility and resources, foundations are capable of devising innovative work arrangements that could become models within the labor force.

Foundation work, for all the strain of meeting career and home responsibility, has the potential to offer a real niche of opportunity for women struggling with these problems. If it cannot remove the pressure of work-family conflicts, the congeniality and relaxation of bureaucratic routine that foundations can provide, and the easier ambience that workers commented on in earlier chapters, can help them accommodate family pressures.

As Garson (1975) points out, the relaxation of routine and the rearrangement of work schedules can create an ambience that makes all employees, including support staff workers in repetitive, low-interest jobs, much happier about their working situations. Such arrangements and rearrangements, however, can be of only limited help to professional staff who face an open-ended workload in a setting where many high achievers set the pace. Without a serious effort at accommodation in the workplace (introduction of child care centers or child care allotments for women and men parents would be a major step forward), women continue to shoulder the burden of child care arrangements. The political problem of the responsibility of the workplace to the family remains unspecified, and the personal problem of finding adequate care for one's children, and arranging professional-business travel around home responsibilities, belongs to the mother.

Other even larger issues that remain unspecified are the costs and benefits of careerism. Both men and women can deplore the costs of placing all one's emotional energies into one's career. But only women who wish to combine career and motherhood are caught squarely in the dilemma of how to meet both sets of expectations. As long as men can depend upon women to assume the major burden of home and parental care, men can sidestep the problem. In this regard, the world of foundations is just like the world of academia, business, or the professions.

6

Conclusions:
The Paradoxes of
Foundation Employment

Foundations provide their employees with interesting work. Paid grantmakers have the opportunity to learn new things, meet new people, and think about new ideas while on the job. They usually have pleasant working conditions, in an atmosphere where collegiality, informality, and flexibility are prized. It is not surprising, then, that the people we spoke to expressed satisfaction with their jobs.

But foundations have come under increasing pressure as governmental sources of aid have shrunk. More and more proposals for help in philanthropic projects have turned to the private sector. And as opportunities in governmental service for work administering such projects disappear, more and more job applicants turn to the private sector, hoping for employment as well. It is no wonder that many foundation staff members worry over how managing inquiries from both interested potential grantees and recruits requires an increasing amount of time and attention.

The position of women in this context highlights some of the paradoxes of foundation work; for it shows us both the opportunities and the limitations of this field as a setting for employment and advancement. For example, will the gains women have made in the last decade and the move toward professionalism counteract each other? The following discussion presents these paradoxes and what we have learned about them in this study.

One problem for the professional in this field is the realization that there is probably a limited future for careerists in the philanthropic world. First, the career ladder in philanthropy is short. Once one has become the executive of a small private foundation, it is hard to find an equivalent position elsewhere.

The best one can hope for is a parallel move to a similar or a slightly larger foundation. Opportunities are shrinking for movement to government, universities, and other nonprofits, especially in times of policy changes and economic belt-tightening, such as those experienced in recent years. The outlook is complicated further by the growing trend in the foundation field toward professionalization.

Grantmakers, in their concern to rationalize and make more efficient the work that they do, have been greatly concerned with efforts to build professional organization and capability into their work. This tendency may in the future undermine the concept, common in the field, that foundation staff are generalists, that one can come to this work from many different kinds of disciplinary and occupational backgrounds. Up to now, grantmaking employees have benefited from this generalist orientation. Both women and men often report that they came to their work in the foundation by accident, adapted to it very well, and developed expertise and commitment through their experience.

The history of efforts to professionalize shows that one consequence of professionalism is lowered opportunities for women. Studies of women in science and in social reform work (Rossiter 1982; Rosenberg 1982) demonstrate that women have more opportunity in fields that are open to gifted amateurs, not yet developed, or even undesirable. When opportunity develops in an occupational area, or when shrinking opportunities elsewhere make a field seem especially desirable, men have a tendency to replace women. In considering the status of foundation work at this time, then, one concern for women is that professionalization may mean lowered opportunities for them. The position is made more difficult for women as they face, in concert with the men in the field, the problem that any position they achieve may have little transferability.

When occupations become professions, some attempt is generally made to limit opportunities to those already present in the field and to restrict the number of new recruits so that the status and working conditions in the field will not become less advantageous. To the extent that women are already within the existing circle or network, they can participate in this concern for professionalism.

This tendency to restrict entry is always limited, of course, by other avenues into the field outside existing networks. For example, new foundations are formed and the founders, as well as trustees of existing foundations, recruit and select staff from their own networks. But, whatever the future for women in philanthropic work, past history and current problems have led to the paradox that even in an elite occupation, women still make 59 cents on the dollar compared with men.

Some of the differential in pay—and also in titles and authority noted in earlier discussions—may persist because women have taken advantage of accidental opportunities that have made low-level entry possible in the philanthropic arena. Some women in small foundations have risen from secretarial and handmaiden roles to executive positions. As generalists, then, or those who began as amateurs or volunteers, the opportunities for rising to a high position do not also include easy transferability to another type of work setting. Nor does such a rise open up career possibilities in other foundations. It would be interesting to know more about what happens to someone who rises from secretary-clerk to administrator of a foundation as the funds grow, or as the projects under its aegis expand. We do know from our study that women in these positions tend to stay with the foundation where their career rise began. This type of accidental opportunity is different from that which permits mobility in a career pattern outside of one firm or foundation.

The fact that some women are entering the field and are rising in it without referrals, but at lower salaries, suggests that there may be an incipient trend toward the feminization of foundation work, particularly in the smaller foundations. Pressures to hire staff in order to professionalize giving in foundations with modest income lead to hiring individuals, usually women, willing to accept low salary. These women may then gain experience and go on to better-paying positions in other foundations. However, our study suggests that both horizontal and vertical mobility in the present require participation in a special kind of network, in which a background from elite schools and the possession of advanced degrees are important for entry.

Another paradox of foundation work, then, is that the aim for many is social reform, help for the disadvantaged, or the provision of opportunity so that society may become more egalitarian. At the same time, however, the people who provide services are expected to be highly educated and, preferably, from elite schools and backgrounds. Foundations devoted to social equality and solving the problems of society are not able to produce egalitarianism in their own organizations. The irony is that the field prides itself in pathbreaking, but has not been pathbreaking at home. Foundations as yet have no systematic comprehensive programs for innovative child care, or job-sharing, or job-enrichment programs for women and minorities.

Many of these paradoxes are interrelated with the opportunity structure of the foundation community. The notion that individuals can rise, or that women in particular can find a niche of opportunity where they can showcase their skills, is offset by the fact that these niches of opportunity can lead nowhere. If individuals cannot rise out of their own organization, and if the ladder of mobility is limited there, they are not really able to enjoy career mobility. And if the field does offer fewer possibilities, the opportunities for networking within the field and the opportunities to gain visibility in the field also create few job prospects.

The foundation field may be an executive training ground for younger professionals just entering the world of work. There is some evidence in our interviews of individuals who have developed skills and had very satisfying employment experiences. For these people, there seem to be opportunities to rise a level or two, or to switch foundations to take advantage of new positions. Many of the new people are in the 25 to 35 years of age range. If present trends persist, some will work their way up to executive positions or to senior program officer positions before they have to face the end of the career ladder.

At the end of the career ladder the question becomes "What next?" Some people are so content with their work that this question does not arise. They find renewal in the variety of projects, in professional growth, and in sharing their experiences with newcomers to the foundation field or with grantees. For others, with fewer institutional resources or less flexibility, horizons seem limited and discontent is evident. How does one reconcile staying in an interesting, well-paid position that has little growth possibility?

The networking and variety of programmatic and professional organizations that have sprung up in the last ten years may provide a partial answer. Reaching outward, enriching the professional aspects of the field through conferences and seminars, provides growth possibilities for foundation employees. One of the most significant developments is the enormous growth of organizations that serve the administrative, programmatic, and network aspects of foundation work. This reflects professionalism, to a degree. It also serves the initiation needs of newcomers to the field. In our study, for example, we noted the interest of lower-level foundation staff in participation in networks. But it was not clear that such participation would offer them any real advantages for career mobility, although they might find them personally rewarding and interesting. A few individuals might benefit from the increased visibility which networking affords.

It is possible that interaction in networks which include prestigious men would prove helpful, but such opportunities are not generally made available to women. For example, several CEOs at large foundations mentioned the executives' group to which they belonged. However, few women are hired to run large foundations, so this network is not available to most women CEOs.

There are special issues for professionally trained women seeking careers in philanthropy. Their problem is set against the context of opportunities for women in business administration, law, medicine, and the academic professions. These women must consider what their career ladders would have been like had they pursued opportunities in these areas. If they try to enter one of these areas after a period of time in the philanthropic world, they will have failed to keep up with the requirements of another career line: writing for publication, making professional contacts with clients, and so forth. While these can be problems for men as well, women face the additional disadvantages of their relatively recent entrance into the networks of communication, the "old boys' clubs" in which information about jobs may be passed, which can pull them into further career development, either in the philanthropic world or in the profession for which they have been trained.

Throughout our discussion of the work in philanthropy, we have stressed the paradoxes which the employees themselves have called to our attention. Perhaps the most clear paradox in their eyes is that they have some of the powers of philanthropists, but are not themselves rich and powerful donors. A somewhat less stressed theme is that if foundation workers, particularly CEOs, have nominal power to give or withhold grants, it is also true that the board of directors (their employers) has authority over them. Foundation workers have to be sensitive to these paradoxes and be aware of the changing style required for presentation of self as they are facing outward toward the public and potential grantees, and as they face inward in presentation of their views and wishes toward the board of directors.

Some of the subtleties of this kind of interpersonal sensitivity are particularly expected of women in their traditional roles. And so, for example, women who rise through the handmaiden route are expected to be extraordinarily skillful at meeting changing expectations. They need the ability to live with the contradictions. Although they are now directors, or even CEOs, women sometimes work in contexts where some of the board members may remember them as personal secretaries, or even servants. These women learn to walk a fine line, catering to the old-timers and yet meeting the world as executives. One woman we talked to, for example, was expected to bake goodies for board meetings as part of her work as administrator of a small foundation. It seems unlikely that a male in her position would face the same expectation. It is interesting to speculate about what it costs such executives, in terms of their divided or fragmented self-image, to have these two different kinds of expectations focused on them and to be ready to engage in such widely disparate behavior. On the one hand, one might argue that it would create conflict and strain. On the other hand, this set of conflicting expectations might keep such executives closer to the ideas of humility and service stressed by some of our CEO respondents than those who have the appearance of great power and trappings of prestige and authority undiluted with any servitor tasks. The position of such women who have risen through the ranks highlights the problems of any executive who works for a board. All of these CEOs and their staffs will have to spend some time dancing attendance on their boards, even though higher level officers in large foundations have many subordinate staff to whom some of these jobs can be assigned.

The difficulties of maintaining the correct posture are exacerbated by the image that some foundations wish to maintain. For example, the executive may wish to maintain a "radical chic" posture, and yet serve a conservative board. In many of our interviews we received the impression that executives feel that somehow they "manage" their boards. At the same time, they recognize that they must work within the limitations of board expectations. And so executives speak of "educating" or "bringing along" their boards. But they all recognize that they engage in this educational process within the limits of what the board will tolerate. In short, the paradox for the executive is that he or she may appear arrogant and intractable to supplicants and yet have to appear humble or at least tractable to board members. The executive may assume an extremely liberal and reform-oriented posture toward candidates, and yet need to appear conservative and very deliberate or cautious before a board.

Women, more than men, face the paradox of security versus advancement. And in thinking realistically about the structure of opportunities available for them, women are likely to be content with their lot in a way that we may not find so readily among men. For example, those women who rise from hand-maiden to director see their position as one of relative affluence as opposed to relative deprivation. In most studies of relative deprivation (Stouffer *et al.* 1949) men look above them and compare their own lot less favorably with that of those in better positions. But women who have risen from the secretarial ranks are more likely to see how much better off they are than the women they left behind. These upwardly mobile women do not compare their lot with that of other executives who are males and who are better rewarded than the women are. Similarly, as we noted earlier, women in secretarial ranks who do not aspire to upward mobility are relatively content, comparing their lot with that of other secretaries in other kinds of enterprises.

There is a growing ambivalence about the status of women and a stronger tendency among women to compare the lot of a woman professional or administrator with that of a male in a similar position. However, women in the philanthropic world often find it difficult to assess just how fair their salary schedule is and to judge how they should feel about their own position. Their ambivalence and their questioning often arose in interviews, when women wondered if their salary and title were commensurate with what a man might expect if he held their job. Interviewers were sometimes asked their opinion of what expectations were reasonable for salary and title. This may be an indication that women are less self-confident and less assured in their knowledge of the network where consensus arises about appropriate salaries, titles, and promotions in staff positions. But any discontent that women might feel is mitigated by their realization of the limited future for careerists in the philanthropic world. They see the short career ladder in the foundation field and expect it would be even more difficult for them than it would be for a man to find an equivalent job elsewhere, once they have become the director of a small private foundation.

In addition to these problems, women in the foundation world have the problems of any woman careerist wishing to manage a wife and mother role in addition to her work role. As we noted earlier, it is more difficult for women in philanthropic work to marry and have children and also pursue their careers with a high degree of commitment than it is for their male colleagues to do so. Again, new trends in society affect the view of what women can and should expect from their careers. While some women are grateful for part-time or dead-end jobs which permit them to work and also to meet their home responsibilities, more and more women (and some men) are trying to find ways to share career and parenting responsibilities more equally. However, recent research on families—even where wives are aggressive professionals and, in some cases, more successful than their husbands—shows that women bear the major burden of the responsibilities for seeing to it that the children and home are properly cared for (Hertz 1983). Our interviews support this view and suggest that traditional patterns are changing very slowly.

The opportunities of the philanthropic world, then, may be most satisfying for these women with families who are happy with the flexibility and perquisites that are available for program officers and administrative assistants, and the opportunities that can be constructed for part-time or flexitime work in either of these categories. These opportunities allow women to participate in the world of employed work while managing home and child care. But they are not opportunities that would appear desirable, or even acceptable, to many men.

Some limitations and prospects (in situations where some ambiguities prevail) for women seem unlikely to change in the near future. For example, bright women who rise from relatively low positions as secretaries or research assistants to high positions in foundations often have to face the innuendoes of their rise. As Rossiter (1982) points out in her book on women scientists, women who are rewarded for their work by patrons or mentors are seen as receiving a gift rather than the appropriate reward for meritorious effort. When rewards are gifts rather than earned "rights," the innuendoes about such women carry an unpleasant and unprofessional overtone. Any bright woman, under the mentorship of a male, has to fight against the suspicion that she is a pet or a "sweetie" of a powerful patron. Whether or not such an aura clings to the rise of a woman in the philanthropic world, she has the problem of transferability that already exists in foundation work, compounded by the notion that her position is acquired as a gift rather than as a right. It is not surprising that women in these ambiguous circumstances have problems of self-image and self-confidence. Of course, these problems are exacerbated by working in a situation where credentials are not clearly required.

It is not apparent how to find the most deserving and competent foundation employee because it is not clear that any special set of skills is required to learn these jobs. People are often picked idiosyncratically or highhandedly by boards of trustees because of prior friendships or family connections. Some of these people do very well. Other people just "fall" into their jobs through some accident or prior work experience. And some of these people do very well. Our informants showed no consensus about what background and training best prepare someone for the work of foundation executive. And looking at the array of informants, we find them from a wide variety of backgrounds—both in training and in prior experience.

Finally, the ambiguities for women are made more difficult by the fact that the work is very often carried out in conjunction with the wishes of rich people. That means that even the most powerful, well-connected, and dignified of CEOs has to spend some time in social or quasi-social attendance on a board which expects to do its work within a kind of social ambience. The CEO is expected to understand the requirements and expectations of the board, and to meet them, sometimes before an explicit request has been directed. If, in addition to these general, structural problems, women executives have to deal with traditional boards holding rather conventional notions of how women behave, the work can have some great difficulties despite its rewards.

This study of career trajectories and opportunities tells us more than just what advantages and limitations await those who chance to find positions in foundations. The shifting, sensitive, and ambiguous relation of philanthropy to the local community as well as to society at large, the delicate balance between professional staff and board perspectives, the maintenance of more or less hierarchical relations within the staff structure—all these issues are made clearer for us by examining the position of women and men in foundations. In the largest view, then, we hope our study informs the reader about problems and prospects for the future of foundations, whatever the distribution of women and men who staff them.

Appendix 1
Statistical Analysis
of Salary Data

Analysis of Data

Summary

Statistical analysis of aggregate salary data for foundation CEOs and program officers indicates that salary level is significantly correlated with the size of foundation assets, educational level, gender, and length of service of incumbents. In almost all cases, however, the average salaries of women are lower than those of men, even when the effects of education and other variables are controlled.

Introduction

Aggregate salary data from the 1982 *Compensation and Benefits Survey (CB Survey)* were used in the analysis. This biennial survey was sent to 1,280 foundations who are members of the Council on Foundations and related regional associations of grantmakers. Responses were received from 429 foundations, which represent 44 percent of the assets and 39 percent of the grants in the field. The CEO and program officer positions were the specific ones analyzed, although some tests included all professional positions (omitting clerical and support positions).[1]

The nature and extent of this survey impose limitations on the findings presented here. The respondents do not constitute a random sample, although

---

[1] All statistics were computed using the *Statistical Package for the Social Sciences* (Nie et al. 1975).

they are representative of the field. In addition, since the survey was designed for other purposes, some useful information—for example, age and years in the workforce—was not collected. Finally, the foundation field is a small one; sometimes there are too few cases for in-depth analysis. While these limitations must be kept in mind when reviewing the findings, the overall pattern is persuasive. Monetary rewards are significantly greater for those who work in the largest organizations, who have Ph.D.s, J.D.s, or M.D.s (among CEOs), and who are male. In the following pages, factors that influence salary levels are discussed and statistical results are presented.

Framework for the Analysis

A preliminary model of factors that are likely to have a bearing on salary levels was constructed. It included structural variables that indicate the level of foundation resources (asset size, grants amount, number of staff) and individual attributes of employees (highest educational degree and field of study, gender, minority status, years in the organization, and years in the position. See Chart 1 for a list of the variables).

Questions posed in the analysis were:

1. Which variables are significantly associated with salary levels of individuals in foundation work? Is gender among them?
2. How much of the total variance in salary level is explained by these variables? Is gender a significant factor?
3. What is the average difference between male and female salaries after adjusting for other factors? Is the difference significant?
4. Do these salary differentials vary by size of foundation assets?

Prior work and observation led to the expectation that salary level would be positively related to the size of the organization, educational level, and length of service, and negatively related to female gender.

Cross-tabulation and Correlation

Asset, salary, grants, and length of service data were grouped into ranges and contingency tables were prepared. Inspection of these tables revealed the distribution and properties of the data as well as associations between variables. For example, there were too few minority persons to permit analysis along that dimension, and the data for the variable on CEOs' previous positions had so many missing cases that it also was excluded from further analysis.

While the data clearly showed the influence of an organization's resources on the salary level, analysis of the CEO position was limited by the fact that only two women were CEOs in the largest foundations in the sample. While this fact in itself indicates that there are limited opportunities for women at that level, detailed analysis of the relationship of salary and gender within this asset group was not possible.

So few program officers work in the smallest foundations that detailed analysis was also limited for this position in certain asset groups. It was further complicated by the fact that there are hierarchies of program officers in the largest foundations (asset group 1), but not in the smaller foundations. Table 15 shows average salary by position and foundation size. For the purposes of this analysis, all program officers were included as one group. Men predominate at the top of the program officer hierarchy, and so it is not surprising that they show higher average salaries than women.

Pearson's product moment correlations were computed separately for CEO and program officer positions and jointly for all professional positions below CEO. Those results are presented in Table 16. Variables associated with the resource size of the foundation were most strongly correlated with salary, followed by educational level, gender, and number of staff in the organization.

Product moment correlations for program officers show a similar pattern, but the correlation coefficient for salary and gender is slightly stronger than that of salary and asset group. Length of service is also significantly related to salaries. Having established that salary level is significantly correlated with organization size, gender, length of service, and educational level, the next step was to examine the nature of these relationships.

First, an analysis of variance was computed. Then, to make the analysis more concrete, a T-Test was used to compare average salaries of men and women while controlling for the effects of the independent variables.

Analysis of Variance (ANOVA)

The multiple classification version of analysis of variance was performed to estimate the average difference in salary level for men and women when other variables such as asset group, education, and length of service are introduced as controls. The analysis was performed individually for each position, first using asset group as a factor, then within each asset group, and finally ignoring asset groups altogether.

For CEOs, the salary differential between men and women is $27,000 before the effects of asset group, education, years in position, and years in the organization are introduced as controls. When the effects of those variables are controlled, the salary differential is $9,390. The effects of gender are significant at the .008 level, while asset group and education are significant at the .000 level. The factors in the model explain about 63 percent of the variation in salary. (Table 17 presents ANOVA results for CEOs.)

If the same analysis is conducted excluding asset group 1 (because there are so few women in that group), the results are similar. The difference in salary level between men and women CEOs is $16,440 before controlling for the other variables, and $10,270 after controlling for them. Gender is significant at the .004 level in this calculation.

Conducting the same analysis within each asset group (except for asset group 1), we see a similar pattern. In asset group 2 the difference in salary levels between men and women is first $26,510; after controlling for other variables, it is $19,390. Gender is significant at the .005 level. Within asset group 3, the difference in salaries between men and women is $5,170 before and $4,180 after controlling for other variables. Gender is not significantly (.2) related to salary level within this group, and the explained variation of the model is not significant. A similar pattern is evident within asset group 4. Mean salary difference between men and women is $9,670 before controlling for other variables, and $5,590 after controlling for them. The effects of gender are barely significant in this case (.086), but the explanatory power of the model is significant.

Gender explains more of the salary variation among the larger foundations than among the smaller ones when the effects of education and length of service are controlled. If asset group is not brought into the analysis at all, the $27,220 mean salary difference between men and women is reduced to $19,050 (rather than $9,390) by controlling for education and length of service. Both gender and education are significant at the .000 level, while years in position and years in the organization are not significant. Gender is responsible for 12 percent of the explained variation in salary if asset group is controlled for in the analysis, but for 25 percent of the variation if it is not. Within asset groups, gender accounts for 32 percent of salary variation in asset group 2, 13 percent in asset group 3, and 22 percent in asset group 4.

Among CEOs, after the effects of education and length of service are controlled, the relationship between gender and salary level is more pronounced in larger foundations than in smaller ones. The gender-salary relationship is also more intense when asset group is omitted from the analysis. By not controlling for asset size, the full extent of the distribution of female CEOs within the field is considered. The $19,050 salary differential clearly shows that women generally occupy the lower-paid executive positions in the field.

For program officers, multiple classification analysis using gender and asset group as independent variables and length of service indicators as covariates also shows a significant relationship of the independent variables to salary. Looking at the whole group, gender accounts for 34 percent of the variation, and asset group for 37 percent of the explained variation. The total model explains 46.5 percent of the salary variance and is significant at the .000 level. There is an $11,260 difference between mean salaries of men and women after the effects of length of service and asset group are considered (see Table 18).

Within asset group 1, adjusted variation attributable to gender is 40 percent and amounts to $13,000 compared with $15,630 before adjusting for length of service. Gender, years in the organization, and years in position are all related to salary at the .000 level. The model accounts for 31 percent of the salary variation.

Within asset group 2, gender is significantly related to salary but length of service is not. Gender accounts for 27 percent of the variation and results in a

$5,460 salary differential between men and women, virtually the same as when length of service is not controlled ($5,440).

In asset group 3, length of service is more significantly related to salary than is gender, but the effect after controlling for covariation is to increase the proportion of variation related to gender (17 to 32 percent) and to increase the salary differential attributable to gender, indicating that women with significant years of service receive lower salaries, while men receive higher salaries. In asset group 4 there are too few men to compare. When the calculation is made excluding asset group 1 data, the effect of gender increases after adjusting for asset group and length of service. The salary differential increases from $5,370 to $6,050, and gender is significant at the .000 level.

If program officer salaries are computed without regard to assets of the foundation, 34 percent of the salary variance is explained by gender and length of service. Of that amount, 45 percent is related to gender. Before taking account of length of service, the salary difference due to gender is $16,410; afterward it is $14,870. Gender is significant at the .000 level. In most of the cases discussed, the factors in the model explain a significant proportion of salary variance. Within the model, gender is a significant factor in explaining the difference in salary levels.

T-Test

The T-Test provides a descriptive measure that indicates whether or not there are true differences between groups. This test is analogous to the analysis of variance, but comes at the problem from a slightly different vantage point and provides concrete measures of differences at each level. The analysis of variance (ANOVA) estimates average effects for gender differences while the T-Test calculates gender differences for each level of the control variable.

Mean salaries and significance levels were first calculated separately for each independent variable in the analysis, then for each variable after controlling for the others. For example, mean salaries for men and women CEOs are $62,700 and $31,500, respectively. The difference in the means is significant at the .000 level. The salaries of men and women who have been in the organization for less than five years, however, is $54,300 and $38,400. Although this is less of a difference, it is still significant at the .008 level. There is even more of a difference between average salaries of men and women CEOs who have been in their organizations for five years or longer: $66,800 and $35,900. The difference in these salaries is significant at the .000 level. A comparison of educational levels reveals similar patterns for CEOs. Average salaries for women with a B.A. education or less is $35,400, while for men it is $48,600—a difference significant at the .008 level. The difference is even greater at the master's 'level. Average salaries for men are $60,900, while they are $34,700 for women, sigificant at the .000 level. There is still a difference in salaries at the Ph.D. level: $77,800 for men and $52,200 for women. But this difference is less significant at .064 (see Table 19).

Without relating these variables to one another, they suggest that women who have been in organizations less than five years have salaries more comparable to their male colleagues than those who have been in organizations longer They also suggest that master's degrees do not affect women's salaries as much as men's, and that a Ph.D. or an equivalent law or medical degree has the most impact in terms of reducing the salary differential for women.

When these same comparisons are made within asset groups, controlling for length of service and education at the same time, the difference in mean salaries between men and women is somewhat blunted. Comparisons are not possible in asset group 1 because of the few women CEOs in that group. In asset group 2, differences in salaries between men and women are still apparent, but the significance level is between .04 and .07. In asset group 3, for the cases where there are available data, the differences in salary levels are not significant. In asset group 4, there are not significant salary differences between men and women with a B.A. education or less who have been in the organization less than five years. But there are significant differences between men and women at both the B.A. (males $44,000 and females $24,000) and M.A. (males $35,800 and females $21,900) levels who have been in their organizations for five years or longer (see Table 19b).

The figures illustrate concretely the findings already mentioned in the section on ANOVA. Women who have run the smallest foundations for many years are paid salaries that are significantly lower than men in similar positions. Women who have entered the field more recently are earning salaries more comparable to their male colleagues, although salaries for women still tend to be lower. At all levels among CEOs, women's salaries are less than men's, but at some levels education and length of service blunt the significance of gender.

T-tests of the mean salary difference between men and women program officers are significant at the .000 level (men $46,900 and women $31,000). Controlling for years in the organization narrows the gap for those employed less than five years (men $40,200 and women $30,000), but widens the gap for those employed more than five years (men $53,200 and women $33,000). Both differences are also significant at the .000 level (see Table 20).

When asset group and years in the organization are considered together, the differences in average salaries decrease. As we might expect, in asset group 1, where hierarchies of program officers are common, salary differences between men and women are significant at the .001 level for those who have been in the organization less than five years (men $44,400 and women $34,400) and at the .000 level for those with over five years of service (men $54,700 and women $37,700).

Paradoxically, in asset group 2, there is a more significant salary differential (.06) between men ($30,100) and women ($25,300) with less than five years of service than between men ($34,100) and women ($26,300) with more than five years of service (significance .12). As in asset group 1, it is also notable that the average salary for women with more than five years of experience is less than that of men with fewer than five years of experience.

In asset group 3, the salary differential for men ($34,400) and women ($24,800) with less than five years of service is significant at the .038 level. Comparisons in asset group 4 are not possible because of the limited number of cases.

Gender is clearly significantly related to salary level among program officers. While adding length of service and asset groups has an impact, these do not negate the significant effects of gender.

Conclusions

The analysis indicates that gender is related to salary level and usually at a significant level. The factors included in the analysis account for a significant amount of the salary variation, and within the model, the relationship of gender and salary remains strong, even when the effects of other variables are controlled. That is, women on the average receive lower salaries than men, and factors that might account for those differences, such as education, length of service, and size of the organization, within this model, do not completely do so.

Table 13. Number and Gender of CEOs by Foundation Asset Size

	Female		Male		Total	
Asset Group	Number	Percent of Asset Group	Number	Percent of Asset Group	Number	Percent of Total
Group 1	2	6	34	94	36	19
Group 2	18	29	44	71	62	34
Group 3	15	33	31	67	46	25
Group 4	14	34	27	66	41	22
Total	49	27	136	73	185	100

Table 14. Number and Gender of Program Officers by Foundation Asset Size

	Female		Male		Total	
Asset Size	Number	Percent of Asset Group	Number	Percent of Asset Group	Number	Percent of Total
Group 1	87	39	135	61	222	69
Group 2	49	72	19	28	68	21
Group 3	14	64	8	36	22	7
Group 4	8	89	1	11	9	3
Total	158	49	163	51	321	100

CHART 1

Variables Used in the Analysis
(Compensation and Benefits Survey Data)

1. Asset Groups:
   1 = $100 million and over in assets or $5 million or more in grants
   2 = $25–$99 million in assets or $1.25 to $4.99 million in grants
   3 = $10–$24.9 million in assets or $500,000–$1,249,000 in grants
   4 = Under $10 million in assets or less than $500,000 in grants

(Operating foundations are placed into asset groups by multiplying operating and grants budget by 20.)

2. Educational Level:
   1 Undergraduate degree or less
   2 Master's degree or graduate work
   3 Ph.D., J.D., M.D., D.D., and other equivalent doctoral degrees

3. Years in Position/Organization:
   1 = 0–2 years
   2 = 3–5 years
   3 = 6–9 years
   4 = 10 years or more

   For some analyses: 1 = 0–4 years; 2 = 5 years or more

4. Chief Executive Officer (CEO): President, Executive Director, Director, Vice President, Administrator, and other titles

5. Program Officer: Program Director, Program Officer, Program Associate, Assistant Program Officer

6. Other Executive/Professional Positions:
   Vice President
   Officer, Secretary, Treasurer
   General Counsel
   Investment Officer
   Assistant Officer
   Controller
   Assistant and Associate Director, Assistant to President
   Research Professional
   Information and Communications Officer
   Librarian
   Office Manager, Business Manager
   Computer Manager
   Other professionals: doctors, lawyers, social workers, etc.

Table 15. Average Salary for Men and Women by Position and Foundation Size

Position	Women	Men	Ratio
Asset Group 1			
Chief Executive	**	$100,809	**
Senior Program Officer	$48,477	61,278	.79
Program Officer	36,247	47,807	.76
Program Associate	28,330	38,308	.74
Other Executive/Professionals	36,626	56,412	.65
Clerical Staff	17,249	20,692	.83
Asset Group 2			
Chief Executive	41,129	67,889	.61
Senior Program Officer	**	41,384	**
Program Officer	27,525	30,111	.91
Program Associate	21,607	**	**
Other Executive/Professionals	28,096	40,440	.69
Clerical Staff	16,162	18,476	.87
Asset Group 3			
Chief Executive	36,150	41,557	.87
Program Officer	32,163	31,694	102
Program Associates	21,625	**	**
Other Executive/Professionals	22,008	34,943	.63
Clerical Staff	14,902	13,700	109
Asset Group 4			
Chief Executive	25,025	35,147	.71
Program Officer	22,600	**	**
Other Executive/Professionals	16,684	25,750	.65
Clerical Staff	13,034	13,131	.99

** 2 or fewer cases.

Table 16. Pearson Product Moment Correlations

Position/Salary Variable	Pearson Coefficient	Significance Level
CEO		
Asset Group	.6433	.001
Grants Paid	.6120	.001
Number of Staff	.2429	.001
Female Gender	.3631	.001
Educational Status	.4183	.001
Years in Position	.0754	.154
Years in Organization	.0580	.217
Program Officer		
Asset Group	.4310	.001
Female Gender	.4961	.001
Years in Position	.2970	.001
Years in Organization	.3611	.001
Professionals (Excluding CEOs)		
Female Gender	.4536	.001
Asset Group	.3918	.001
Years in Organization	.1777	.001
Years in Position	.0976	.006

NOTE: The Product Moment Correlation measures the strength of a relationship between two variables. It varies between +1 and −1.

Table 17. Analysis of Variance in Salary Level of CEOs: Multiple Classification Analysis

a. Variation Attributable to Gender, Asset Groups, and Educational Level with Covariates Years in Position and Years in Organization.

Variation Attribute	Number	Unadjusted Variation	Adjusted Variation
Gender (.008 significance)			
Male	134	7.070	2.440
Female	47	−20.150	−6.950
		(.36)*	(.12)*
Asset Groups (.000)			
Group 1	36	42.810	38.030
Group 2	59	4.520	4.720
Group 3	45	−17.110	−15.070
Group 4	41	−25.310	−23.640
		(.73)*	(.66)*
Educational Level (.000)			
B.A. or less	63	−13.120	−6.070
M.A. and equivalents	63	−3.680	−4.530
Ph.D., J.D., M.D., and equivalents	55	19.250	12.140
		(.40)*	(.24)*

$R^2 = .626$
Grand Mean = 56.710

b. Within Asset Group 2, Variation Attributable to Gender and Educational Level with Covariates Years in Position and Years in Organization.

	Number	Unadjusted Variation	Adjusted Variation
Gender (.005 significance)			
Male	43	7.190	5.260
Female	16	−19.320	−14.130
		(.44)*	(.32)*
Educational Level (.004)			
B.A. or less	17	−9.260	−6.610
M.A. and Equivalents	25	−7.560	−6.570
Ph.D., J.D., M.D., and equivalents	17	20.380	16.270
		(.49)*	(.39)*

$R^2 = .331$
Grand Mean = 61.320

c. Within Asset Group 3, Variation Attributable to Gender and Educational Level with Covariates Years in Position and Years in Organization.

	Number	Unadjusted Variation	Adjusted Variation
Gender (.202) significance)			
Male	30	1.720	1.390
Female	15	−3.450	−2.790
		(.16)*	(.13)*
Educational Level (.066)			
B.A. or less	22	−4.570	−4.940
M.A. and equivalents	12	−2.160	2.970
Ph.D., J.D., M.D. and equivalents	11	6.800	6.640
		(.31)*	(.32)*

$R^2 = .138$
Grand Mean = 39.600

Table 17. *(continued)*

d. Within Asset Group 4, Variation Attributable to Gender and Educational Level with Covariates Years in Position and Years in Organization.

Variation Attribute	Number	Unadjusted Variation	Adjusted Variation
Gender (.086 significance)			
Male	27	3.300	1.910
Female	14	−6.370	−3.680
		(.39)*	(.22)*
Educational Level (.195)			
B.A. or less	17	−2.890	−1.090
M.A. and equivalents	14	.130	−1.910
Ph.D., J.D., M.D., and equivalents	10	4.740	4.530
		(.25)*	(.22)*

$R^2 = .271$
Grand Mean = 31.400

e. Variation Attributable to Gender and Educational Level with Covariates Years in Position and Years in Organizations.

Gender (.000 significance)			
Male	134	7.070	4.950
Female	47	−20.150	−14.100
		(.36)*	(.25)*
Educational Level (.000)			
B.A. or less	63	−13.120	−11.000
M.A. and equivalents	63	−3.680	−3.090
Ph.D., J.D., M.D., and equivalents	55	19.250	16.140
		(.40)*	(.34)*

$R^2 = .232$
Grand Mean = 56.710

NOTES: * Eta and beta statistic.
  a. Salary differences attributable to gender decline from $27,220 to $9,390 when adjusted for the independent variables (asset group and education) and covariates.
  b. Within asset group 2, differences attributable to gender decline from $26,510 to $19,390 when adjusted for education and covariates.
  c. Within asset group 3, gender does not have a significant effect on salary level (.202), but the difference in salary levels attributable to gender is reduced from $5,170 to $4,180 when adjusted for education and covariates.
  d. Within asset group 4, the relationship of gender to salary differences is somewhat significant. Salary differences attributable to gender are reduced from $9,670 to $5,590 when adjusted for education and covariates.
  e. Salary differences attributable to gender decline from $27,220 to $19,050 after effects of the independent variable (education) and covariates are considered, without regard to asset size.

Table 18. Analysis of Variance in Salary Level of Program Officers: Multiple Classification Analysis

a. Variation Attributable to Gender and Asset Groups with Covariates Years in Position and Years in Organization

Variable	Number	Unadjusted Variation	Adjusted Variation
Gender (.000 significance)			
Male	158	8.230	5.650
Female	159	−8.180	−5.610
		(.50)*	(.34)*
Assets Groups (.000)			
Group 1	215	5.650	4.100
Group 2	71	−11.890	−8.230
Group 3	22	−8.660	−7.190
Group 4	9	−19.860	−15.590
		(.51)*	(.37)*

$R^2 = .465$
Grand Mean = 39.110

b. Within Asset Groups, Variation Attributable to Gender with Covariates Years in Position and Years in Organization.

Asset Group 1			
Gender (.000 significance)			
Male	129	6.250	5.200
Female	86	−9.380	−7.800
		(.48)*	(.40)*

$R^2 = .314$
Grand Mean = 44.750

Asset Group 2			
Gender (.012 significance)			
Male	20	3.910	3.920
Female	51	−1.530	−1.540
		(.27)*	(.27)*

$R^2 = .103$
Grand Mean = 27.210

Asset Group 3			
Gender (.051 significance)			
Male	8	2.430	4.580
Female	14	−1.390	−2.620
		(.17)*	(.32)*

$R^2 = .464$
Grand Mean = 30.440

Asset Group 4			
Gender			
Male	1	—	—
Female	8	—	—

Table 18. (*continued*)

c. Variation Attributable to Gender with Covariates Years in Position and Years in Organization (Disregarding Asset Groups)

Variable	Number	Unadjusted Variation	Adjusted Variation
Gender (.000 significance)			
Male	158	8.230	7.460
Female	159	−8.180	−7.410
		(.50)*	(.45)*

$R^2 = .342$
Grand Mean - 39.110

d. Variation Attributable to Gender and Asset Groups (excluding Asset Group 1) with Covariates Years in Position and Years in Organization

Gender (.000 significance)			
Male	29	3.840	4.330
Female	73	−1.530	−1.720
		(.25)*	(.29)*
Asset Groups (.000)			
Group 2	71	.010	.260
Group 3	22	3.240	2.060
Group 4	9	−7.960	−7.100
		(.29)*	(.24)*

$R^2 = .225$
Grand Mean = 27.210

NOTES: * Eta and beta statistic
  a. Gender is a significant variable in this model. Salary differences attributable to gender are reduced from $16,410 to $11,260 when adjusted for the effects of asset groups and covariates.
  b. Gender is significantly related to salary within asset groups, though the relationship is strongest in the largest foundations. Adjusting for covariates reduces the salary differential between males and females in asset group 1, has little effect in asset group 2, and increases the difference in asset group 3.
  c. If asset group is disregarded, the salary differential attributable to gender is reduced from $16,410 to $14,870 when adjusted for covariates, rather than to $11,260 as happens when asset groups are included in the analysis. Ignoring the effect of asset groups intensifies the effect of gender.
  d. When asset group 1 is excluded from the analysis, gender accounts for $5,370 before adjustments for the effects of asset groups and covariates, and $6,050 after adjustments are made.

Table 19. T-Test Analysis of Differences in Mean Salaries of Male and Female CEOs

a. Differences in Mean Salaries Controlling for Asset Group and Length of Service

Variable	Average Salary	Men	Women	Significance
(Overall)	$56,400	$62,700	$36,500	.000
All Asset Groups				
Less than 5 years		$54,300	$38,400	.008
5 years or more		$66,800	$35,900	.000
Asset Group 1	$99,500	$100,800	*	—
Less than 5 years		$83,400	*	—
5 years or more		$107,100	*	—
Asset Group 2	$61,100	$66,400	$41,100	.000
Less than 5 years		$67,200	$35,300	.0025
5 years or more		$66,000	$43,400	.003
Asset Group 3	$39,600	$41,600	$36,200	.119
Less than 5 yrs.		$40,900	$36,700	.279
5 years or more		$41,900	$38,200	.279
Asset Group 4	$32,200	$33,900	$25,000	.0025
Less than 5 years		$28,600	$28,300	.469
5 years or more		$37,800	$23,200	.0001

b. Differences in Mean Salaries Controlling for Asset Group and Education Level

All Asset Groups				
B.A. or less		$48,600	$35,400	.008
M.A. or equivalent		$60,900	$34,700	.000
Ph.D., M.D., J.D., or equivalent		$77,800	$52,200	.064
Asset Group 1				
B.A. or less		$83,800	*	—
M.A. or equivalent		$91,500	*	—
Ph.D., M.D., J.D., or equivalent		$112,900	*	—
Asset Group 2				
B.A. or less		$57,400	$44,300	.028
M.A. or equivalent		$62,400	$35,100	.006
Ph.D., M.D., J.D., or equivalent		$81,700	*	—
Asset Group 3				
B.A. or less		$37,800	$30,100	.088
M.A. or equivalent		$42,800	$40,300	.320
Ph.D., M.D., J.D., or equivalent		$45,600	*	—
Asset Group 4				
B.A. or less		$32,300	$24,300	.081
M.A. or equivalent		$34,900	$25,500	.088
Ph.D., M.D., J.D., or equivalent		$37,000	*	—

Table 19. (*continued*)

c. Differences in Mean Salaries Controlling for Asset Group, Educational Level, and Length of Service

Variable	Average Salary	Men	Women	Significance
Asset Group 1				
B.A. or less				
Less than 5 years		*	*	—
5 years or more		$83,800	*	—
M.A. or equivalent				
Less than 5 years		$74,300	*	—
5 years or more		$101,300	*	—
Ph.D., M.D., J.D. or equivalent				
Less than 5 years		$90,700	*	—
5 years or more		$122,100	*	—
Asset Group 2				
B.A. or less				
Less than 5 years		$53,200	*	—
5 years or more		$60,100	$45,400	.037
M.A. or equivalent				
Less than 5 years		$55,500	$34,800	.041
5 years or more		$65,300	$35,400	.074
Ph.D., M.D., J.D., or equivalent				
Less than 5 years		$90,000	*	—
5 years or more		$78,000	*	—
Asset Group 3				
B.A. or less				
Less than 5 years		$34,900	$29,200	.260
5 years or more		$38,700	$35,300	.389
M.A. or equivalent				
Less than 5 years		$38,300	*	—
5 years or more		$46,100	$40,000	.192
Ph.D., M.D., J.D., or equivalent				
Less than 5 years		$47,500	*	—
5 years or more		$44,100	*	—
Asset Group 4				
B.A. or less				
Less than 5 years		$26,400	$24,200	.369
5 years or more		$44,000	$24,300	.037
M.A. or equivalent				
Less than 5 years		*	*	—
5 years or more		$35,800	$21,900	.023
Ph.D., M.D., J.D., or equivalent				
Less than 5 years		$36,500	*	—
5 years or more		$37,300	*	—

*2 or fewer cases

Table 20. T-Test Analysis of Differences in Mean Salaries of Male and Female Program Officers Controlling for Asset Group and Length of Service

Variable	Average Salary	Men	Women	Significance
Overall	$39,400	$46,900	$31,000	.000
Years in Organization				
Less than 5 years	$34,600	$40,200	$30,000	.000
5 years or more	$45,700	$53,200	$33,000	.000
Asset Group 1	$44,600	$50,300	$35,400	.000
Less than 5 years	$39,000	$44,400	$34,400	.001
5 years or more	$50,400	$54,700	$37,700	.000
Asset Group 2	$28,400	$31,100	$25,700	.025
Less than 5 years	$28,100	$30,100	$25,300	.063
5 years or more	$29,000	$34,100	$26,300	.120
Asset Group 3	$30,400	$32,900	$29,100	.230
Less than 5 years	$29,000	$34,400	$24,800	.038
5 years or more	$34,300	*	$36,800	—
Asset Group 4	$19,200	*	$19,800	—
Less than 5 years	$17,500	*	$18,000	—
5 years or more	$25,200	*	*	—

*2 or fewer cases

Table 21. CEO Salary by Organizational and Personal Characteristics (Partial Correlations)

Salary by Gender Controlling for	Correlation Coefficient	Significance
Asset Group	.3019	.001
Grants Paid	.3226	.001
Number of Staff	.3468	.001
Education	.2900	.001
Years in Position	.3523	.001
Years in Organization	.3567	.001

NOTE: Partial correlations measure the amount of variation explained by one independent variable (in this case gender) after the others have explained all they can. The coefficients here indicate that the effect of gender is still significant when each of these variables is controlled.

Table 22. Salary of Foundation Personnel by Organization and Personal Characteristics (Multiple Regressions)

Position/Variables	Beta	F
CEO (1)		
Asset Group	.640	150.12
Female Gender	.232	19.45
Years in Organization	.033	.15
Years in Position	.035	.17
$R^2 = .528$		
Standard error = 22,968		
F = 50.26		
Program Officer		
Asset Group	.328	54.84
Female Gender	.362	66.08
Years in Organization	.219	15.09
Years in Position	.101	3.18
$R^2 = .434$		
Standard error = 12,056		
F = 60.60		
Other Professional		
Asset Group	.290	39.82
Female Gender	.362	63.01
Years in Organization	.118	4.09
Years in Position	.022	.14
$R^2 = .286$		
Standard error = 20,599.9		
F = 37.31		
All Professionals Above		
Asset Group	.283	93.01
Female Gender	.381	171.45
Years in Organization	.079	3.96
Years in Position	.099	6.17
$R^2 = .287$		
Standard error = 20,933		
F = 88.42		
CEO Position (2)		
Grants Paid	.532	93.12
Female Gender	.152	7.18
Educational Level	.293	27.30
Number of Staff	.072	1.80
Years in Position	.124	1.68
Years in Organization	.039	.17
$R^2 = .528$		
Standard error = 23,238.6		
F = 31.9		

NOTE: Beta = standardized partial-regression coefficients; F = test statistics; R^2 = the proportion of variance in the dependent variables explained by the set of independent variables; Standard error = on the average, the deviation of predicted from actual salaries in the model.

The multiple regressions above show that the independent variables predict a significant proportion of the variance in salaries for each case above, but that these variables are better predictors of CEO salaries (R^2 indicates that 52.8% of variance is explained) than of Program Officers (R^2 = 43.4%) or other professionals (R^2 = 28.6%). For CEOs, asset group predicts the greatest variation in salary (Beta .640), while for Program Officers, gender predicts the greatest variation (Beta .362). In all cases gender is a significant predictor of salary within the context of the model.

Appendix 2

Career Patterns in Philanthropy

Interview Guide

1. Will you briefly describe the goals and major programs of the foundation?

2. What is your position title?

3. How long have you been in the position?

4. How long have you been employed by the foundation?

5. How did you obtain your present position?

6. Were you looking for a foundation position?

7. Were you familiar with the field?

8. How many people work at the Foundation?
   Full-time:
   Part-time:

9. In addition to staff, do you use consultants?
   Would you give a few examples?

10. What is the table of organization?
    (CEO) How many employees report directly to you?
    a. How does your position fit into the overall personnel structure?
    b. Who do you report to?
    c. Do you have supervisory responsibilities?

11. What are the position titles of those people who report to you?

12. Do you have a formal written job description?

13. Does it reflect the work that you are currently doing? (If not, how is it different?)

14. What are your major responsibilities in this position?

15. How would you rank these responsibilities in terms of importance?

16. Do you delegate any of these responsibilities?   (To whom? How often?)

17. Do you have a role in formulating the budget? (If so, what?)

18. Do you have investment responsibilities?

19. What are the steps in a standard proposal review process? (evaluation, screening, writing synopsis, technical assistance, soliciting proposals, field visits, interactions with grantseekers, board presentations)

     Describe your last proposal review process. How did it go?

20. Do you need to work with other staff members? (Who? How do you generally get along? Do you have the support of your supervisor?)

21. Tell me how you prepare for a typical board meeting. (How many members are there? Do you have a special rapport with any members? Do you ever see board members individually? Characterize your relationship—under what circumstances? or What is the nature of the interaction?)

22. Does your job provide you with the opportunity to interact with peers in the foundation field? (Formal, informal? Phoning, meetings?)

23. Do you belong to organizations which help facilitate such interaction? (Examples?)

24. Are you regularly in touch with other foundation staff members for informal advice and assistance? (mentor, role model)

25. Do your responsibilities involve high visibility?
     (For example, do you make public appearances or give speeches?)

26. Which three job responsibilities consume most of your time?

27. How many hours do you usually work each week?
     (Do you take work home? Evenings? Week-ends? Time-off? Extra pay?)

28. Does your job require entertaining or social engagements?
     (Does the foundation pay for these expenses?)

29. Does the foundation pay for professional development? (Examples?)

30. What benefits are provided by the foundation?
     (health insurance, retirement, perks)

31. What are the things you like best about your job?

32. What are the things you like the least?

33. If it were possible, how would you improve your current job?

34. How does this position fit in with your career goals?
     (What did you want to be as you were growing up?)

35. In the course of your career have you ever depended upon an individual
     or groups of individuals for advice and encouragement? (Have you had a
     mentor? What do you do when you have trouble with your work? If yes,
     was this person or group within the foundation field or elsewhere?)

36. How important is this person or persons to your current job?

37. Does your personal or family situation have a bearing on your work or
     your career options?

     How does your family/ do those closest to you/ feel about your work?

38. How many people live in your household?

39. Do you have children? (How many? Ages? Do they live with you? Do you
     have child care assistance?)

40. Do you have domestic help?

41. What do you do in your leisure time?

42. What is the highest level of education that you have completed?

Degree	Year Obtained	Institution	Major Field
Some			
Undergrad.			
Graduate (M.A.)			
Ph.D.			
M.D.			
J.D.			
Other Prof.			

43. Do you plan to obtain any further formal education?

44. Briefly describe your previous positions, beginning with your last job. Please include dates, title, name of organization, location, full- or part-time status, and major responsibilities.

Date	Title	Organization	Location	Full-time Part-time

45. How does your current job compare with others that you have held?

46. Are you involved in volunteer activities?

47. Describe your current volunteer activities.

Date	Title	Organization	Location

48. Did you engage in volunteer activities in the past?

49. Would you briefly summarize some of those activities?

50. How did your background prepare you for your current position?

    As you look back over your own history, what do you think has been most helpful?

51. What would you consider the ideal combination of education and experience for this position?

52. Do you plan to continue in foundation work?

53. What opportunities or limitations do you see for yourself in this job or in the field?

54. How would you describe the future of the field?

Personal Information Sheet

55. Gender: Female _____   Male _____

56. Age: Under 30 _____

                 31–40 _____

                 41–50 _____

                 51–60 _____

                 61–70 _____

                 Over 70 _____

57. Race: Asian American _____

                 Black _____

                 Hispanic _____

                 White _____

                 Other (please specify) _____

58. Nationality: In addition to being an American, from which nationality groups (Irish, Italian, German, Japanese, etc.) are you mainly descended? _____

59. Religion: What is your present religion, if any? (Please be specific. For example, are you Catholic, Jewish, Baptist, Mormon, or what?) _____

60. Marital Status: Never married _____

                 Married _____

                 Unmarried, but living with a mate _____

                 Separated _____

                 Divorced _____

                 Widowed _____

                 Other (please specify) _____

61. If you are now married or have been married, please describe your spouse's main occupation. _____

_____

62. Write in your annual salary _____ (or check the figure that comes closest to your own salary last year).

            Under $10,000 _____
        $10,000 to 19,900 _____
        $20,000 to 29,900 _____
        $30,000 to 39,900 _____
        $40,000 to 49,900 _____
        $50,000 to 59,900 _____
        $60,000 to 69,900 _____
        $70,000 to 79,900 _____
        $80,000 to 89,900 _____
        $90,000 to 99,900 _____
      $100,000 to 109,900 _____
      $110,000 to 119,900 _____
         $120,000 and over _____

63. Check the figure that comes closest to your total household income last year.

            Under $10,000 _____
        $10,000 to 19,900 _____
        $20,000 to 29,900 _____
        $30,000 to 39,900 _____
        $40,000 to 49,900 _____
        $50,000 to 59,900 _____
        $60,000 to 69,900 _____
        $70,000 to 79,900 _____
        $80,000 to 89,900 _____
        $90,000 to 99,900 _____
      $100,000 to 109,900 _____
      $110,000 to 119,900 _____
         $120,000 and over _____

Appendix 3
Related Philanthropic Groups

Grantmakers in Health
275 Madison Avenue, Suite 1918
New York, NY 10016
(212) 725-0650
Contact: Catherine McDermott

Committee on International Grantmaking
c/o Council on Foundations
1828 L Street, N.W.
Washington, D.C. 20036
(202) 466-6512
Contact: Tom Fox

Precollegiate Education Group
c/o Council on Foundations
1828 L Street, N.W.
Washington, D.C. 20036
(202) 466-6512
Contact: Mary Leonard

Grantmakers Interested in the Arts
c/o New York Community Trust
415 Madison Avenue
New York, NY 10017
(212) 758-0100
Contact: Richard Mittenthal

Grantmakers Interested in the Field of Aging
c/o Charles Stewart Mott Foundation
500 Mott Foundation Building
Flint, MI 48502
(313) 238-5651
Contact: Trudy Cross

Grantmakers Interested in Chemical Dependency
c/o The Kerr Foundation, Inc.
6301 North Western
P.O. Box 13009
Oklahoma City, OK 73113
(405) 842-1510
Contact: Anne Hodges Morgan

Grantmakers Interested in Children and Youth
c/o The Foundation for Child Development
345 E. 46th Street, Room 700
New York, NY 10017
(212) 697-3150
Contact: Jane Dustan

Grantmakers Interested in
  Emergency Loan Fund Programs
c/o Pemberton Management Company
3 Center Plaza
Boston, MA 02108
(617) 451-2100
Contact: Joseph C. K. Breiteneicher

Grantmakers Interested in
  Environmental Issues
c/o Virginia Environmental
  Endowment
700 E. Main Street
P.O. Box 790
Richmond, VA 23206
(804) 644-5000
Contact: Gerald McCarthy

Foundations Interested in Film and
  Video
c/o Maurice Falk Medical Fund
3317 Grant Building
Pittsburgh, PA 15219
(412) 261-2485
Contact: Philip B. Hallen

Working Group on Funding Lesbian
  and Gay Issues
c/o The New World Foundation
100 East 85th Street
New York, NY 02146
(212) 249-1023

Grantmakers Interested in
  Neighborhood Issues
c/o Joint Foundation Support
122 East 42nd Street, Suite 922
New York, NY 10017
(212) 599-0330
Contact: Joellen Lambiotte

Grantmakers Interested in
  Adolescent Pregnancy
c/o Bridgeport Area Foundation
205 Middle Street
Bridgeport, CT 06604
(203) 334-5106
Contact: Ed Keane

Grantmakers Interested in Program
  Focus
c/o Pemberton Management Co.
3 Center Plaza
Boston, MA 02108
(617) 451-2100
Contact: Joseph C. K. Breiteneicher

Foundations Interested in Religion
c/o Foundations and Donors Interested in Catholic Activities
(FADICA)
1730 Rhode Island Avenue, N.W.
Suite 401
Washington, DC 20036
(202) 466-2999
Contact: Francis Butler

Grantmakers Interested in Full
  Economic Employment
c/o The Villers Foundation
1334 G Street, N.W.
Washington, DC 20005
(202) 628-3030
Contact: Ronald Pollack

Grantmakers Interested in Voter
  Education & Registration
c/o Forum Institute
1225 Fifteenth Street, N.W.
Washington, D.C. 20005
(212) 535-9915
Contact: Jeanne Fox

PROFESSIONAL ORGANIZATIONS

Association of Black Foundation Executives
c/o The William and Flora Hewlett Foundation
525 Middlefield Road, Suite 200
Menlo Park, CA 94025
(415) 329-1070
Contact: Hugh Burroughs

Communications Network in Philanthropy
c/o The Duke Endowment
200 South Tryon Street, Suite 707
Charlotte, NC 28202
(212) 535-0400
Contact: Elizabeth Locke

Council on Foundations
1828 L Street, N.W.
Washington, D.C. 20036
(202)466-6512
Contact: James Joseph, President

Hispanics in Philanthropy
c/o James Irvine Foundation
Stuart Street Tower
Suite 2305
San Francisco, CA 94105
(415) 777-2244
Contact: Luz Vega

National Network of Grantmakers
c/o Mary Reynolds Babcock Foundation
102 Reynolda Village
Winston-Salem, NC 27106
(919) 748-9222
George Penick, Co-convenor

Women and Foundations/Corporate Philanthropy
70 West 40th Street
New York, NY 10018
(212) 997-1077
Contact: Joanne Hayes

REGIONAL ASSOCIATIONS OF GRANTMAKERS

Multi-State Associations

Conference of Southwest Foundations
(Serves primarily Arizona, Arkansas, Nevada, New Mexico, Oklahoma, and Texas)
Maud W. Keeling, Executive Secretary
P.O. Box 8832
Corpus Christi, TX 78412
(512) 855-3611

Southeastern Council of Foundations
(Serves primarily Alabama, Arkansas, Florida, Georgia, Kentucky, Louisiana, Mississippi, North Carolina, South Carolina, Tennessee, and Virginia)
Robert H. Hull, Executive Director
134 Peachtree St., N.W., Suite 1100
Atlanta, GA 30303
(404) 524-0911

*Associations currently serving a state
or a multi-county area of the state*

Pacific Northwest Grantmakers Forum
Anne Farrell
c/o Seattle Foundation
1411 4th Avenue Bldg., Suite 1522
Seattle, WA 98101
(206) 622-2294

Council of Michigan Foundations
Dorothy A. Johnson, President
18 N. Fifth St.
Grand Haven, MI 49417
(616) 842-7080

Foundation Forum of Wisconsin
Richard W. Yeo, Managing Director
P.O. Box 11978
Milwaukee, WI 53211
(414) 962-6820

Grantmakers of Western
  Pennsylvania
Kate Dewey, Executive Director
368 One Mellon Bank Center
Pittsburgh, PA 15258

Minnesota Council on Foundations
Jacqueline Reis, Executive Director
1216 Foshay Tower
9th and Marquette
Minneapolis, MN 55402
(612) 338-1989

Northern California Grantmakers
Steve Lieberman, Executive Director
334 Kearny St.
San Francisco, CA 94108
(415) 981-6603

Southern California Association for
  Philanthropy
Lon M. Burns, Executive Director
Eastern Columbia Building
849 S. Broadway, Suite 815
Los Angeles, CA 90014
(213) 489-7307

Greater City Associations

Associated Grantmakers of
  Massachusetts, Inc.
Janet C. Taylor, Executive Director
294 Washington St., Room 417
Boston, MA 02108
(617) 426-2606

Association of Baltimore Area
  Grantmakers
Martha Johnston, Program Officer
Community Foundation of Greater
  Baltimore
6 E. Hamilton St.
Baltimore, MD 21202
(301) 332-4171

Clearinghouse for Midcontinent
 Foundations
Linda H. Talbot, Executive Director
P.O. Box 7215
Kansas City, MO 64113
(816) 276-1176

Co-ordinating Council for
 Foundations, Inc.
Bertina Williams, Executive Director
999 Asylum Ave.
Hartford, CT 06105
(203) 525-5585

Donors Forum of Chicago
Eleanor P. Petersen, President
208 S. LaSalle St., Room 600
Chicago, IL 60604
(312) 726-4877

Rochester Grantmakers Forum
Linda S. Weinstein, Executive
Director
c/o Rochester Area Foundation
315 Alexander St.
Rochester, NY 14604
(716) 325-4353

New York Regional Association of
 Grantmakers
Barrie Pribyl, Executive Director
630 Fifth Ave., Suite 2550
New York, NY 10111
(212) 664-0522

Metropolitan Association for
 Philanthropy
Amy R. Rome, Executive Director
5585 Pershing Ave., Suite 150
St. Louis, MO 63112
(314) 361-3900

San Diego Grantmakers Group
Helen Monroe, Executive Director
c/o San Diego Community
 Foundation
625 Broadway, Suite 1105
San Diego, CA 92101
(619) 239-8815

Bibliography

American Association of University Professors
1983 "The Annual Report on the Economic State of the Profession 1982–83." *Academe*, Vol. 69, no. 4.

Boris, Elizabeth T., and Hooper, Carol
1982 *Compensation and Benefits Report*. Washington, D.C.: Council on Foundations.
1984 *1984 Foundation Management Report*. Washington, D.C.: Council on Foundations.

Boris, Elizabeth T., and Unkle, Patricia A.
1981 *1980 Compensation Survey*. Washington, D.C.: Council on Foundations.

Boris, Elizabeth T.; Unkle, Patricia A.; and Hooper, Carol
1981 *1980 Trustee Report*. Washington, D.C.: Council on Foundations.

Bucher, Rue, and Stelling, Joan G.
1977 *Becoming Professional*. Beverly Hills, Calif.: Sage, pp. 29–37.

Charlton, Joy C.
1983 *Secretaries and Bosses: The Social Organization of Office Work*. Doctoral dissertation, Northwestern University.

Collins, Randall
1975 *Conflict Sociology: Toward an Explanatory Science*. New York: Academic Press.

Coser, Rose Laub
1982 "Stay Home, Little Sheba: On Placement, Displacement and Social Change." In *Women and Work Problems and Perspectives*, edited by Rachel Kahn-Hut, Arlene Kaplan Daniels, and Richard Colvard. New York: Oxford/University Press.

Dykstra, Grechen
1979   *Survey of Community Foundations*. New York: Women and Foundations/Corporate Philanthropy.

Garson, Barbara
1975   *All the Livelong Day*. Kingsport, Tenn.: Kingsport Press.

Hertz, Rosanna
1983   *Dual Career Couples in the Corporate World*. Doctoral dissertation, Northwestern University.

Hughes, Everett C.
1958   *Men and Their Work*. Glencoe, Ill.: Free Press.

Kanter, Rosabeth Moss
1977a *Men and Women of the Corporation*. New York: Basic Books.
1977b *Work and Family in the United States: A Critical Review and Agenda for Policy and Research*. New York: Russell Sage Foundation.

Lofland, J.
1971   *Analyzing Social Settings: A Guide to Qualitative Observation and Analysis*. Belmont, Calif.: Wadsworth.

Margolis, Diane Rothbard
1979   *The Managers Corporate Life in America*. New York: Morrow.

Marting, Leeda
1976   "What We Now Know . . . What We Need to Do." Women and Foundations, unpublished report.

McPherson, J. Miller, and Smith-Lovin, Lynn
1982   "Women and Weak Ties: Differences by Sex in the Size of Voluntary Organizations." *American Journal of Sociology* 87:4.

Merton, Robert K.; Fiske, Marjorie; and Kendall, Patricia
1956   *The Focused Interview*. Glencoe, Ill.: Free Press.

Nason, John W.
1977   *Trustees and the Future of Foundations*. New York: Council on Foundations.

Nie, Norman H.; Hull, C. Hadlai,; Jenkins, Jean G.; Steinbrenner, Karin; and Bent, Dale H.
1975   *Statistical Package For the Social Sciences*. New York: McGraw-Hill.

Odendahl, Teresa, and Boris, Elizabeth
1983a "A Delicate Balance: Foundation Board-Staff Relations." *Foundation News*, 24:3. Washington, D.C.: Council on Foundations. pp. 34–45.
1983b "The Grantmaking Process." *Foundation News*, 24:5. Washington, D.C.: Council on Foundations. pp. 22–31.

Odendahl, Teresa; Palmer, Phyllis; and Ratner, Ronnie
  1980   "Comparable Worth: Research Issues and Methods." In *Manual on Pay Equity*, edited by Joy Ann Grune. Washington, D.C.: Committee on Pay Equity.

Ostrander, Susan A.
  1984   *Women of the Upper Class*. Philadelphia: Temple University Press.

Rosenberg, Rosalind
  1982   *Beyond Separate Spheres*. New Haven: Yale University Press.

Rossiter, Margaret W.
  1982   *Women Scientists in America: Struggles and Strategies to 1940*. Baltimore: Johns Hopkins University Press.

Selden, Catherine; Mutare, Ellen; Rubin, Mary; and Sacks, Karen
  1982   *Equal Pay for Work of Comparable Worth: An Annotated Bibliography*. Chicago: American Library Association.

Simmel, Georg
  1955   *Conflict and the Web of Group-Affiliations*. New York: Free Press.

Stouffer, S. A., *et al.*
  1949   *The American Soldier: Adjustment During Army Life*. Vol. 1. Princeton, N.J.: Princeton University Press.

Treimann, Donald J., and Hartmann, Heidi I., eds.
  1981   *Women, Work, and Wages: Equal Pay for Jobs of Equal Value*. Washington, D.C.: National Academy Press.

U.S. Census Bureau
  1983   *Money Income of Households, Families, and Persons in the U.S.* Series P-60. Washington, D.C.: U.S. Government Printing Office.

U.S. Department of Labor, Bureau of Labor Statistics
  1983   *Employment and Earnings*. Vol. 30. Washington, D.C.: U.S. Government Printing Office.

Wilensky, H. C.
  1964   "The Professionalization of Everyone?" *American Journal of Sociology*, 70:2, pp. 137–58.

Yankelovich, Skelly and White, Inc.
  1982   *Corporate Giving: The Views of Chief Executive Officers of Major American Corporations*. Washington, D.C.: Council on Foundations.

Zurcher, Arnold J., and Dustan, Jane
  1972   *The Foundation Administrator: A Study of Those Who Manage America's Foundations*. New York: Russell Sage Foundation.

Index